HISTORIC
HAUNTS
OF
ST. LOUIS

JENNIFER ELWYN

Haunted
America

Published by Haunted America
A Division of The History Press
Charleston, SC
www.historypress.com

Cover images: Eads Bridge. *Photo by Angela M. Fulks*; view looking down Clamorgan Alley with Eads Bridge and Gateway Arch in the distance. *Photo by Angela M. Fulks.*

First published 2024

Manufactured in the United States

ISBN 9781467158060

Library of Congress Control Number: 2024938203

CONTENTS

ACKNOWLEDGEMENTS

I want to thank my parents for instilling a sense of curiosity in me at an early age. I would accomplish nothing without curiosity. Thanks to Lacey Reinhardt, who has been a wonderful friend and a lady who drags me into situations I wasn't planning to get myself into. Rachel Woods, thank you for reading the draft and cheering me on when I wasn't feeling so confident. Thank you to Angela Fulks for the beautiful photos. To the wonderful people at the Missouri Historical Society Library, thank you for being patient, insightful and just as excited as me to look at a map from 1823. And to anyone who has waited for me to finish this book so I can do whatever it is I promised you I would do, thank you for your patience.

INTRODUCTION

I grew up in a small town along the Mississippi River. Actually, we call it an island. Kaskaskia Island is a unique place since it is a town in Illinois on the Missouri side of the river. Kaskaskia is not just special because it is on the wrong side of the river but rather because it was the first capital of the state of Illinois. Of course, that city now technically rests at the bottom of the river, and we have a Native American curse to explain why it was swallowed by the Mississippi. My family never shied away from sharing stories of curses, hauntings, aliens and even the elusive MoMo Monster (Missouri Big Foot) when I was a kid. So, it isn't surprising that one day I would become a paranormal investigator.

Back then, I would have never imagined living in a city as large as St. Louis. Most of what I knew of the city was confined to the occasional school field trip to the zoo or the Gateway Arch. Other than that, the city was a foreign place to me. When I moved here in 2011, I was starting over (much like the people in the stories that follow) and looking for a better life. I had officially started investigating the paranormal the previous year and was excited to explore the old buildings in my new city. It took time, but I eventually found a great team of investigators and relish the idea that I get to interact with history in such a unique way.

When I was younger, I thought that history was a boring subject foisted on us in school, but now I see how all of these individual stories connect, weaving a tapestry of life that affects how we experience our world today. As you read through the stories in this book, you may notice the points where each one connects. Many names appear in various stories, and certain places affect individuals in different ways. It took becoming a paranormal investigator for me to fully appreciate history. I now walk into locations and begin to think about the people who preceded me. I wonder what they thought and felt the first time they opened that front door. I think about how privileged I am to be able to continue their story.

If you ask paranormal investigators what makes a place haunted, they will likely tell you that it's complicated. While tragic incidents are often associated with hauntings, it is also common to find strange happenings in places with no tragedy at all. It is believed that, over time, people leave a mark on the places they inhabit. This makes hauntings a collection of days, weeks, months and years of life that passed through a location. At the heart of every haunting, you will find people who are going about their lives and trying their best to make ends meet. St. Louis is full of hauntings not just because of the myriad tragedies that have happened over the years but also because of the people who came here looking for a better life.

CHAPTER 1

ESTER CLAMORGAN

Eighteen years after a French merchant named Pierre Laclède Liguest landed on the bluff just downriver from the confluence of the Missouri and Mississippi Rivers, Jacques Clamorgan arrived in the town of St. Louis (1781). At that time, there were three unpaved streets running parallel to the Mississippi River placed high enough from the river's edge to safeguard from flooding. The main streets were crossed with smaller streets, and tidy wooden homes populated the town. Beyond that was prairie land (common fields) where the residents planted crops and pastured livestock.[1] Like many others before and after him, Jacques saw the opportunity that lay beyond those mud-covered streets.

Before arriving in St. Louis, Jacques had become adept at dealing in any commodity that could lead to profit but struggled with the basic concept of paying back his debts. He spent time in the West Indies and in St. Pierre, where he found himself owing a substantial amount of money to people who had supported his early dealings. Since he was unable to pay this money back, he fled to New Orleans, with his debtors following close behind. As his debtors were closing in, he fled again up the Mississippi River and arrived in St. Louis.[2] It was here that Jacques believed he could set up a home that allowed him to trade anywhere the river would take him. It also would make it easier for him to be somewhere else when debtors came looking for him.

In 1784, he purchased his first piece of land in St. Louis. It was this same year that Jacques received an enslaved frontier woman by the name of Ester as settlement for a debt. Ester was around the age of thirty-one and had

Metal plate identifying Clamorgan Alley located on the sidewalk along Morgan Street between First and Second Streets. *Author's collection.*

a daughter by the name of Siley who had to be left behind. In June 1785, Jacques agreed to purchase twelve-year-old Siley for $550 and brought her to St. Louis to join her mother. This is the point in the story when tales get romanticized, but the story of Ester and Jacques Clamorgan was not a love story. While they were reported to be lovers, it was purely a physical relationship. Jacques was seen abusing Ester during her stay in his home, and while there was a time when this appeared to be less frequent, it still proved that Jacques had little respect for Ester. Meanwhile, Ester oversaw the household while Jacques often traveled to conduct business. She never learned to read or write, but she was fluent in French and could speak a bit of Spanish. She managed the other slaves, various boarders and visitors who noted that she appeared to be in charge of the home.[3]

On July 14, 1793, Ester became a free woman when Jacques signed paperwork showing that she had paid him the $500 of her original purchase price through "faithful services." He also agreed to pay her $50 each year she continued to work for him. Ester then negotiated for the transfer of Siley to her ownership, and a contract was made detailing that Siley would receive her freedom upon her mother's death.[4]

At first, granting Ester her freedom appeared to be a noble gesture, but Jacques saw this as an opportunity to shield himself should his assets be seized. While Jacques had become a successful man, he still tended to find himself in debt far more often than he would have liked. At this time, a free person could petition for, buy and hold land. Four days after she was freed, "Ester" was approved to buy a lot adjoining Jacques's home. In September, "Ester's" petition for the purchase of another lot next to Clamorgan's home was approved. In October, "Ester" was awarded roughly sixty-seven acres north of town, and in November, Jacques sold a parcel of land to "Ester" for farming.[5] Of course, Ester knew nothing of these transactions, as they were all done in her name by Jacques Clamorgan.

Sometime between 1795 and 1797, Ester left Jacques's home due to escalating tensions that had led to the abuse of Ester and her daughter, Siley. When she left, Ester took not only her family's belongings but also certain papers that included her manumission, her deed to Siley and the manumission for her grandson (Edward) and mixed into these papers were the documents giving Ester the land purchased in her name. While Ester could not read the documents, she recognized her name and knew that they were important to her and her family. On August 23, 1798, Ester purchased a lot on what is now Church Street for twenty dollars and quickly set about building a home for her family. Over the years, she would purchase additional tracts of land and become a strong, independent woman with a faithful community of friends. Ester eventually agreed to work for Jacques on occasion but never moved back into his home.[6]

Meanwhile, Jacques invited a succession of African American "wives" into his bed. Much like his relationsihp with Ester, these were not love-filled unions but instead consisted of deceit, threats, abuse and trickery to get what he wanted out of the women. While the specifics of Jacques's ancestry are not fully known, it is believed that he came from a mix of Welsh, French, Portuguese and African ancestors. With this background, Jacques was more accepting of having mixed-race children and fathered four children born to three different enslaved women working in his home. At birth, each child was baptized, and Jacques had the priest make a notation in the registry that each child was free from the moment of their birth. In 1809, Jacques took additional steps to ensure the freedom of his children by signing deeds of emancipation for St. Eutrope (1799), Apoline (1803), Cyprian Martial (1803) and Maximin (1807), ensuring that his creditors would be unable to claim his children as assets. He also transferred land to each of them to further guarantee that they would not be destitute when he died.[7]

Despite the name on the deeds, Jacques always treated Ester's land as his own, and in 1806, he began the process of trying to get the claims transferred to himself. When authorities asked why the land was in Ester's name, Jacques admitted that it had been originally granted to Ester but that she had since given it to him. Jacques would need to convince officials of the transfer, so he began to explore ways to create the documents he needed. Meanwhile, Ester was happily working in the Clamorgan home and caring for his children along with Jacques's current "wife," Julie.[8]

Detail of 1823 map showing Ester Clamorgan's property located along Oak/Morgan between Third and Second Streets. *Courtesy of the Missouri Historical Society, St. Louis.*

In 1807, Jacques was away for business in Mexico when Ester contracted smallpox. She had been caring for Jacques's children and unfortunately spread the disease within the household. Once well enough, Ester tried her best to aid the ill and had physicians to the house daily. While all of the children recovered, Jacques's favorite "wife," Julie, died. When Jacques returned and was told of the death, he became enraged with Ester. Not only was he grieving the loss of Julie, but he was also in financial distress and on the verge of bankruptcy.[9] He saw Ester's land as the only means of getting himself out of his current situation. It was at this time that Ester learned of her legal rights to the land.

Jacques produced multiple fraudulent deeds in order to prove his claim to her land, including one stating that Ester had sold her daughter, Siley, back to him. This would make any of Siley's children slaves (except Edward, whose freedom was on record) belonging to Jacques. Ester turned to lawyer William C. Carr for help and handed over all of the documents she had available. Carr told her that he would proceed with the lawsuit on two counts: (1) that Jacques had illegally tried to deed Ester's property to himself, and (2) that Jacques had withheld the fifty dollars per year he had promised to pay her when she was freed. As payment for his work, Carr would receive one of her town lots. In 1810, Carr sold one of Ester's lots to Jacques, and other questionable transactions were eventually discovered. Ester's land had been transferred to multiple people in the town without her knowledge. By 1811, Carr had abandoned Ester's case and did not return any of her documents.[10]

Jacques Clamorgan died in 1814, but that did not end Ester's attempts to reclaim her land. She no longer trusted many of the powerful people around her and began to solidify her claims so she could protect her family from future problems. In May 1817, she had a deed drawn up freeing every member of her family. Under Missouri law, any children born to a formerly enslaved person would be free as well, and thus Ester ensured the freedom of her descendants long after her death. While working for Jacques, Ester learned the value of land and accumulated her own tidy nest egg of plots in and around St. Louis. To further safeguard her family, Ester put into trust two town lots in Alton, Illinois, and a lot in St. Louis on the corner of Fifth and Myrtle for her granddaughter Teresa. With her family now protected, Ester decided to once again attempt to recover the land Jacques took from her. She made a deal with attorney Isaac McGirk in which he paid her one dollar for a half share of three land grants she had received. He agreed to bear all the expenses involved in reestablishing her rights to the land, and if successful, he would be granted one-half of Ester's real estate. McGirk quickly realized that the case was far more complicated than he had initially expected and that he was unlikely to be successful.[11]

Next Ester hired lawyer Gustavus A. Bird to take up her case, which included suing her former lawyer William C. Carr. Since Carr was now a judge in the St. Louis Circuit Court, her case was transferred to St. Charles Circuit Court. During the trial, Carr claimed that Ester had produced all the necessary documents proving her claims and that all she cared about was keeping her family safe. He stated that she had never asked Jacques for any of the land and that she didn't want anything that was to be taxed so Carr offered to take all of the land as payment for his services. He later sold the land as was within his legal rights. In terms of her back wages, Carr stated that he had given Ester everything that he had received from Jacques. Bird presented copies of deeds that were suspected to be forgeries and stated that at least one individual who had signed as "witness" claimed to have never signed such a document. Unfortunately, this witness died before the trial. As the land had been sold multiple times since Jacques's initial forgery, the transaction timeline became murky, and on May 15, 1833, the case was dismissed.[12]

Ester died on August 28, 1833, at roughly the age of eighty. In 1841, her granddaughter Teresa, along with her husband, George, continued the legal fight by filing cases against William C. Carr and Peter Chouteau, hoping to reclaim the land that had once belonged to their family. Their lawyer, Thomas M. Knox, brought the case before the Missouri Supreme Court in 1842, but it went nowhere. Finally, in 1848, George, Teresa and Ester's granddaughter Agatha accepted $10,000 from William C. McElroy for all their rights to Ester's claims with the understanding that McElroy would pursue the claims at his own expense and that if he was able to secure any money for those claims, he would pay them half.[13] This would never come to pass.

Today, the land that belonged to both Jacques Clamorgan and Ester looks a bit different. While the streets still exist, there are now granite cobbles that were laid in the 1870s. The buildings have also changed. Jacques, Ester and the other inhabitants in St. Louis had lived in wooden structures, and in 1849, a large fire wiped out everything along the riverfront.[14] The buildings were replaced with limestone and brick structures that still stand today. Despite these changes, occasionally people see a strange dark-skinned woman who doesn't quite fit among the renovated and modernized buildings. She can be seen walking slowly from Morgan Street to Lucas Avenue and then around the block as if surveying the area. On at least one occasion, she was seen relaxing on a bench only to disappear moments later. While on a tour, one couple stopped to snap a photo in front of a large window in one of the older buildings, later finding a strange woman standing just behind them. Could this be Ester keeping an eye on her property and waiting for the time when someone will finally give her back what was hers?

CHAPTER 2
THE OLD COURTHOUSE

When people think about St. Louis, many things come to mind: the St. Louis Cardinals, the Gateway Arch, beer, music and crime. St. Louis has won the unfortunate title of "Most Dangerous City" more times than we can count. While the vast majority of the population is just trying to live an honest life, there has always been a contingent of scoundrels in our midst. These individuals are more than happy to lie, swindle and even take by force whatever they like. That is why places like the Old Courthouse came to be essential to a rapidly growing population with a mixed interest in obeying the law. Of course, even building a structure focused on justice would require a few suspicious dealings with questionable people. It would also become the site of many controversial and sometimes tragic cases that highlight how we have altered the meaning of "criminal" over time.

In 1805, the newly appointed justice of the Territorial Superior Court, John B.C. Lucas, arrived in St. Louis. Lucas was often described as an intelligent but ill-tempered man who was politically incorruptible. He believed in law and order and could be very uncompromising when he determined that something went against his standard of "right." These traits would cause him more than a few headaches in St. Louis. The city was home to traders and men accustomed to making fast and sometimes questionable deals in the harsh wilderness to the west. Before arriving in St. Louis, Lucas was active in arguments against large land speculators and chaired the committee tasked with separating Louisiana into the territories of Louisiana and Orleans. The

1803 Louisiana Purchase led to a reevaluation of all land titles granted by the French and Spanish authorities, and Lucas was suspicious of some of the larger land claims as he believed they may have been fraudulent. With a seat on the Board of Land Commissioners, Lucas voiced his concerns about existing Spanish land titles.[15] Of course, this led him to have issues with one of St. Louis' "first citizens," Auguste Chouteau.

Auguste Chouteau and his stepfather, Pierre Laclède, are often referred to as the founding family of St. Louis. In 1763, Laclède (with the aid of Chouteau) was tasked with an expedition up the Mississippi to establish a trading post at the confluence of the Mississippi and Missouri Rivers. Finding the land too marshy, they moved down the river, selecting a site along the bluffs for the post and a new town to be named St. Louis.[16] Due to its location, St. Louis would quickly become a key location in the fur trade.

As a smart and calculating man, August Chouteau was known as someone who could drive a hard bargain. He excelled in his clerk position at the St. Louis trading post, where he displayed a talent for business and an ability to form relationships with even the most difficult traders. Chouteau had a strong relationship with members of the Osage Nation and had earned favor with the Spanish officials who governed Louisiana. With the support of these two groups, Chouteau was able to dominate the fur trading industry and expand the family business, which eventually included vast amounts of real estate. The 1803 Louisiana Purchase agreement created problems for Chouteau as he worried that his land titles might not be confirmed. He did his best to curry favor with the incoming American authorities and was mostly successful. Unfortunately, this did not reduce the threat posed by people like John B.C. Lucas, who were firm in their desire to fully explore the legality of the land claims held by individuals such as Chouteau. Chouteau regularly held public meetings to protest the government's limitations on Spanish land claims and thus became a problem for Lucas.[17]

With this history, most wouldn't be surprised to learn that Chouteau and Lucas were not friends. What they would find surprising is that Chouteau and Lucas made their own land deal. They agreed to set aside their differences for the benefit of the growing city. In the early days of St. Louis, government business was often conducted in places such as the Baptist church, a tavern and even at the old Spanish fort. While this may have worked for a much smaller population, it would eventually become very clear that more people meant more crime. The city needed a place to hold court and not just for criminals but to settle legal matters such as land contracts, wills, debts and more. In 1816, the rivals agreed to donate land to build a courthouse. They signed a deed stating that the land was to be "used forever as the site on which the Courthouse of the County of St. Louis should be erected."[18]

It would take ten years for construction to begin on the brick courthouse, and Auguste Chouteau would die one year after its completion in 1828. The completed courthouse had a total of nine rooms and one large courtroom that was adequate for a city of 5,500 residents. Unfortunately, by the late 1830s, the city of St. Louis had almost tripled in size, and so had the court's needs.[19]

In 1838, the city held a contest to solicit designs for a new, larger courthouse. While prizes were awarded, it was determined that none of the designs was suitable for the city's needs, and instead, Henry Singleton was selected as the architect for the project. He planned to construct a stone and brick building that would fill the entire city block. It would have four wings that rotated around a central rotunda and was designed in such a way that it could be completed in sections, expanding as the city needed space. It also allowed construction costs to be spread over time and preserved the original structure while construction was ongoing.[20]

Work on the new structure began on October 21, 1839, with a ceremony to dedicate the new building. A procession of Masons, Odd Fellows, Hibernians and the St. Louis Grays marched together down the two blocks between the Masonic Hall and the construction site. When they arrived, they placed several items in the cornerstone to serve as a time capsule, including a list of government officers, a dedication ceremony program, a copy of each of the city newspapers and various coins. This cornerstone was eventually lost during the long construction project.[21]

Henry Singleton quickly began construction of the west wing of the building but soon found himself having to contend with a variety of problems that would slow the project. As with any construction project, the workers often complained of long hours and low wages, but more concerning were the supply issues. Deliveries of brick and stone were regularly late, not in the correct quantity or of inferior quality for the price. Local politicians routinely reviewed the construction plans and made edits to the interior arrangement of the building, causing more delays. Then there were the funding problems. The tolls collected on country roads, license fees and landowner tax were not sufficient to maintain the project. Eventually, the court had to obtain loans from wealthy St. Louisans at a 10 percent annual interest rate. In 1840, the original stone contract was terminated, and the court agreed to utilize a limestone quarry north of St. Louis leased for $250 per year. Singleton then arranged for his brother-in-law to supervise the quarry operations, and the construction problems began to smooth out.[22]

Later that year, concerns were raised about the amount Singleton was being paid to supervise the project. At $3,000 per year, some thought that they could reassign the project to someone else to save money. Judge James Purdy began to circulate rumors about Singleton implying a lack of integrity, fraudulent accounting practices, using county funds to speculate on land deals and plans to drain the county treasury of its funds. A private accounting firm audited Singleton's books in November 1841 but found nothing of concern. Despite this, Judge Purdy continued his plan to oust Singleton and tried to convince him that the other court justices were planning to terminate him. Singleton considered resigning but instead decided to seek additional funds to accelerate the construction project—funds the court did not have. So, on January 15, 1842, the court fired Singleton as a cost-cutting measure and hired William Twombly for $1,200 per year. Additional cost-cutting measures included closing the limestone quarry operation and reducing the number of workers on site.[23]

Twombly likely did not realize what he had gotten himself into as he accepted his position to supervise not just the courthouse project but also the new jail. As part of his agreement, he was required to revise the jailhouse plans to further reduce costs. While Twombly did change the plans for the jail, the cost did not go down. He quickly became embroiled in a scandal regarding inferior ironwork sold to him by a friend. After a very short nine-month term of employment, William Twombly was fired, and Judge Purdy assumed control of both projects.[24]

Despite all of this drama, construction continued, and offices began moving into the west wing in April 1842. The circuit court moved into the lower west wing courtroom in 1843. More grumbling about extravagance and costly construction followed the move as this courtroom took up most of the west wing, had floor-to-ceiling windows, fluted columns, massive railings, a lofty ceiling and forty-four wooden desks that wrapped in a semicircle around one side of the room. It left reporters asking who might have paid for such an elaborate space or if the court had gone into debt creating it.[25]

The centerpiece of the courthouse update was the beautiful rotunda that opened on February 22, 1845. The citizens took a break from complaining about the cost of the building and instead marveled at its polished limestone flooring, granite pillars, oak columns, gilded oil lamps and the skylight in the center of the dome that allowed sunlight to spread down into the building. Attendance estimates range from three to four thousand people, and every newspaper commented on the vast numbers of people filling the two upper galleries, the stairs, the ground floor and even the alcoves.[26]

An 1851 photo of the Old Courthouse before demolition of the original building. *Courtesy of the Missouri Historical Society, St. Louis.*

In 1847, the St. Louis courthouse's lower west wing courtroom became the scene of one of the most historic trials in its history: the Dred Scott trial. Dred Scott was an enslaved man who was owned by Dr. John Emerson of Missouri. Emerson was a military surgeon who served at various military locations between 1833 and 1842. Dred Scott accompanied Emerson to these posts and found himself residing in the free state of Illinois and the Wisconsin Territory, where slavery was prohibited. During their stay at Fort Snelling (now in the state of Minnesota), Scott met and married Harriet Robinson. Emerson then purchased Robinson so she could remain with Scott. In 1842, Emerson and his wife returned to Missouri, where Emerson later died. Scott attempted to purchase his freedom from Emerson's widow but was denied. He then sought the aid of antislavery lawyers who argued that due to Scott's move to the free state of Illinois, Scott and his wife were technically free. They lost their first trial but were granted a second trial. In 1850, the state court in St. Louis declared Scott free.[27]

Unfortunately, two years later, the verdict was reversed by the Missouri Supreme Court. Scott was eventually given to John F.A. Sanford, brother

DRED SCOTT.

Wood engraving of Dred Scott created by Holcomb. *Courtesy of the Missouri Historical Society, St. Louis.*

of Emerson's widow, who resided in New York State. Due to the change of jurisdiction, Scott's lawyers proceed with litigation against Sanford in federal court. The case was eventually heard in the U.S. Supreme Court, where Judge Taney ruled that African Americans were not and could never be citizens of the United States. In addition, the ruling stated that the Missouri Compromise of 1820, which declared territories west of Missouri and north of latitude 36°30' as free, was unconstitutional. Further, it concluded that having lived in a free state did not grant Scott his freedom since he was essentially personal property. This verdict, along with a rapidly changing political environment, would set in motion a series of events that eventually led to the Civil War. As for Scott, he was purchased in 1857 by the Blow family, and they granted Scott and his wife their freedom.[28]

While Scott's case made its way through the courts, a new architect was hired for the courthouse project, Robert Mitchell. The original brick courthouse building was demolished in 1852, and construction of the east wing began shortly thereafter. The east wing would house the Probate Court, where property settlements and wills would be decided. As seen in the Scott case, prior to the Civil War, slaves were considered property and could be included in cases of bankruptcy or contested wills. In several instances, the east steps of the courthouse were used as a public auction site, with enslaved people auctioned alongside other assets. While historians are unsure how many people were sold in this way, many ads for these auctions can be found in the papers of the day. Across the hall from the Probate Court was the County Court, where freed slaves had to obtain an official license to remain in the state of Missouri. Being an expensive document to obtain, many chose to leave Missouri instead.[29]

While attempting to move the construction of the courthouse along, Mitchell began work on the south wing in 1853. Unfortunately, issues with the ceiling sagging in the lower west wing courtroom (completed ten years earlier) made renovations to this section of the building necessary and added unforeseen costs to the project. In order to support the structure, the large courtroom was split into two smaller courtrooms with a hallway between them. This new configuration would better support the ceiling and reduce the chance of future issues.[30]

In 1857, Mitchell was accused of not paying carpenters and took to the papers to argue that it was not his responsibility to pay the workers. That responsibility fell on the contractor, Mr. Joseph Foster. Arguments over construction costs continued, new taxes were levied and the citizens of St. Louis continued to comment on the never-ending construction and costs. Six years after accepting the position with the courts, Mitchell resigned. He was succeeded by Thomas Lanham, who quickly became the subject of controversy regarding mismanagement of the courthouse project. Lanham's brother was a justice on the County Court and owned the construction firm contracted for the work on the building. Judge Lanham would become embroiled in his own controversies, one of which involved reportedly fraudulent signatures to appropriate funds for improving roads in the jurisdiction in which he resided. Another was for suppressing an investigation of ballot stuffing during the August 1858 election. While Judge Lanham was able to hold on to his position, Thomas Lanham was dismissed from the courthouse project in 1859.[31]

Twenty years after the start of construction, William Rumbold became the final architect for the courthouse project. It was this same year that the *Daily Missouri Republican* newspaper noted that the unfinished state of the courthouse had become "the theme of constant ridicule, regarded as a huge unsightly deformity, by our citizens, and impressing strangers with an unfavorable opinion as to the energy and good taste of our people." Government officials were determined that the courthouse had to be finished as quickly as possible and hoped that Rumbold was the man to do it.[32]

The most contentious time in Rumbold's tenure as architect was during the design of the iron dome set to adorn the top of the building. The previous architect, Thomas Lanham, had submitted a design for the dome that appeared to be much stronger than Rumbold's airy design. Understanding the average St. Louisan's penchant for needing proof that something will work, Rumbold decided to build a scale model of the dome and then placed thirteen thousand pounds of iron on the top proving that it would be stronger than the other, much heavier design. His design won over the citizens and the court. The dome was completed in April 1861, and he went on to patent his design in 1862.[33]

It was decided that the magnificent new dome necessitated an update to the interior of the rotunda to match its grandeur. To do this, a new balcony

PHOTOGRAPH OF THE MODEL OF DOME

OF THE

St. Louis Court House,

Under a *test weight* of nearly 13,000 pounds of pig iron, taken the fourth day after loading. Model weighed 150 pounds.

Present at the loading: Hon. H. J. LIGHTNER, Presiding Justice County Court; Col. A. R. EASTON, Justice County Court; Dr. WILLIAM TAUSSIG, Justice County Court; SAMUEL W. EAGER, Clerk County Court.

Patented June 17th, 1862.   WILLIAM RUMBOLD, *Architect.*

William Rumbold's strength test model of the Old Courthouse dome, 1862. *Courtesy of the Missouri Historical Society, St. Louis.*

was added, and local artist Charles Wimar was brought in to paint murals. Wimar was a German American painter known for his murals depicting Indian and colonial life. Unfortunately, by the time Wimar took the job, he was seriously ill. Stories from the time suggest that he had to be carried up to his platform each day and that a mattress was placed on nearby scaffolding allowing him to rest occasionally. With the assistance of his half-brother, August Becker, Wimer painted four oval "lunette" paintings on the fourth level of the rotunda and four allegorical figures higher in the dome. The lunettes depicted the British-Indian attack on St. Louis, the founding of St. Louis by Laclede and Chouteau, Cochetopa Pass and De Soto discovering the Mississippi in 1541. Each lunette was placed in the cardinal direction to match the location of the scene. As for the allegorical figures of Law, Liberty, Justice and Commerce, they were lost during renovations in 1880, when Ettore Miragoli was hired to retouch the murals. Instead, he painted over the allegorical figures. Thankfully, Miragoli was stopped before he could alter the lunettes. Wimar died at the age of thirty-four in 1862, shortly after completing his work on the courthouse.[34]

Twenty-three years after work began, construction of the courthouse officially ended on July 4, 1862. The final cost of the building was $1,199,871.91. With the country in the grips of the Civil War, the courthouse quickly became host to rallies and soldier recruitment. It was even used as a temporary resting place for ill and wounded soldiers.[35]

After the war, Missouri voters ratified the "Drake Constitution," which formalized the emancipation of the state's enslaved population, established a formal government to replace the provisional Union government and required Missouri male citizens to take an "Iron-Clad Test Oath" to prove their loyalty to the Union before voting in elections. This led to the south wing courtroom, which housed the Missouri Supreme Court, becoming the scene of chaos on June 14, 1865. A group of radicals entered the courthouse to remove all officeholders who refused to take the oath. Six hundred soldiers were stationed outside the building as police were led by the state militia leader, General David Coleman, into the Supreme Court chamber. General Coleman demanded that the justices take the oath. When the justices refused, they were dragged out of the courtroom and charged with disturbing the peace. Three new justices were installed in their place. The test oath was deemed unconstitutional ten years later in 1875.[36]

By the 1920s, the courthouse was once again becoming too small for the needs of the city. Instead of renovating the current structure, it was decided that a thirteen-story courthouse would be built seven blocks to the west.

When the new courthouse opened in 1930, all the offices in the old building were vacated except the magistrate's courts. The vacant rooms were rented to charitable organizations for several years, and the building fell into disrepair. In 1932, the heirs of Chouteau and Lucas sued the city for not using the land as deeded and wanted it to revert to the original owners. Ultimately, the Missouri Supreme Court ruled against them, stating that the original deed did not contain a provision for forfeiture. Instead, the city donated the building to the federal government, and it was to be maintained by the National Park Service. When the park service acquired the building, it was in poor shape, with the ceilings of several rooms in danger of collapsing due to leaks in the roof. Renovations were quickly executed to save the structure, and by 1943 the Old Courthouse had been reopened to tourists.[37]

As one of St. Louis' oldest and most iconic structures, the Old Courthouse has stood as a symbol of justice, hope, freedom, controversy and perseverance despite all odds since 1839. Predating the famous Gateway Arch by more than 125 years, the Old Courthouse building has become the subject of rumors of hauntings for well over a century, making it a place of interest to both historians and paranormal enthusiasts alike.

In 2018, my team had the honor of leading a series of haunted tours of this beautiful building and had the opportunity to speak with employees, who told

St. Louis Old Courthouse, 2024. *Photo by Angela M. Fulks.*

us their stories. Custodians reported feeling a rush of wind pass them by and the hair on their arms stand up when they are near the archival library. An overnight guard once heard footsteps in the rotunda so clearly that the police were called to investigate, only to find the building empty. One courthouse volunteer told us that it isn't uncommon for African American guests to enter the building and break down into tears, saying that they feel the spirits all around them. So, who still walks the halls of the Old Courthouse? Could it be any of the likely hundreds of people who worked on the building? Maybe someone who fought for their freedom within those courtrooms? Is it an architect, checking on the state of his legacy, or Charles Wimar looking for his allegorical paintings? Maybe a wounded soldier or two are still lingering in the hallways. It's hard to say who wanders the building today, but it is very likely that the many people whose life was changed within those walls return occasionally to remind us that the past is very much still alive within.

CHAPTER 3

THE OLD ROCK HOUSE

Often when we build something, we don't always think beyond our own needs. We may ask, "How long will it stand?" but maybe not, "Who will be here when I'm gone?" Buildings, when allowed to stand long enough, have a life of their own and change with the people who pass through the doors. The Old Rock House is a wonderful example of a building that persevered far longer than expected and changed beyond a simple warehouse to become important in the eyes of many St. Louis' citizens.

The land on which the Old Rock House once stood was deeded to Jean Baptiste Trudeau in 1799. Trudeau, a Missouri River explorer, arrived in St. Louis ten years after the city was founded. Once settled, Trudeau became the first schoolmaster of St. Louis and lived above the river in a simple farmhouse. He also owned the property sloping down from his home toward the river so he could utilize the stone quarry. That same year, Manuel Lisa and his wife, Mary "Polly," arrived in St. Louis. Lisa was an ambitious merchant and fur trader who would later come to be known as the "Father of Navigation" on the Missouri River. He would ultimately make thirteen trips up the river and help expand the western fur trade.[38]

Lisa quickly got to work making connections in the city and proving that he could be a very useful member of the community. In 1802, he built a flour mill in exchange for a five-year monopoly on trade to the Osage Indians. In 1807, he traveled up the Missouri River with 42 men on a trading expedition that ended with the building of Fort Raymond. The following year, he formed the St. Louis Missouri Fur Company with now well-known

St. Louis trailblazers like Pierre Choteau Sr., Auguste Chouteau Jr., William Clark and others. In 1809, the fur company set out on an expedition from Fort Raymond with 350 men and built Fort Lisa near what is now Bismarck, North Dakota.[39]

It wasn't until 1810 that Lisa purchased Trudeau's property and his family moved into the farmhouse. Unfortunately, Lisa did not have the luxury of time to devote to his new home. The War of 1812 was creating problems for settlements in the American frontier and thus affecting the fur trade business. The St. Louis Missouri Fur Company was dissolved, and Lisa set out to coordinate with the Native Americans. Having already gained a substantial knowledge of the Native American nations, he was able to keep

Portrait of Manuel Lisa. *Courtesy of the Missouri Historical Society, St. Louis.*

them allied with the Americans rather than the British. This coordination reduced the threat settlements had faced from raids of pro-British tribes. Lisa would later be rewarded for his efforts by being appointed as a U.S. Indian agent by the governor of the Missouri Territory, William Clark.[40]

Lisa returned to St. Louis in 1813 and began construction of a two-story brick home to replace the old farmhouse. He and his family lived on the top floor, and the Lindell brothers rented the first floor for their store. Of course, Lisa was never really settled, and his stay in St. Louis was brief. His work as an Indian agent took him back into Native American territory, where Lisa was well known and trusted by many of the area tribes. In particular, he spent a substantial amount of time with the natives of the Omaha tribe. He eventually married Mitain, daughter of the tribe's chief, in 1814. Mitain and Lisa would go on to have two children, Rosalie and Christopher. You may be asking: wasn't Lisa married? Yes, he was still married to Polly when this union occurred, but this was clearly not a concern for him. Many of the fur traders residing in St. Louis at that time had Native or African American concubines, but rarely did they take them as wives. It was also rare for them to claim the children as legitimate.[41]

In the spring of 1815, Lisa arrived in Portage des Sioux (St. Charles County, Missouri) and brought with him forty-three chiefs and headmen to sign a treaty to end the War of 1812. Through this treaty, the tribes present and the representatives of the United States agreed that "there shall be perpetual peace and friendship" between the citizens of the United States and all the individuals composing the tribe of Sioux and that the peace that existed before the war would be renewed. This treaty also placed the tribes under the protection of the United States and stated that they would hold "the same footing upon which they stood before the late war."[42] Unfortunately, this second part would not be respected by the settlers, and the Native Americans would find themselves being pushed onto reservations.

In 1817, Lisa was living with his Native American wife, Mitain, when he received word that his first wife, Polly, had died. He proceeded back to St. Louis to confirm the care of their son, Manuel Jr., and deal with lingering business. It was shortly after his return in 1818 that Lisa built the warehouse on the levee's edge for his tenants, the Lindell Brothers.[43] This warehouse would come to be known as the Rock House.

In 1819, Lisa married widow Mary Hempstead Keeney and then proceeded to reestablish the Missouri Fur Company with his brother-in-law, Thomas Hempstead. Unlike many women of the time, Mary was interested in her husband's work in Indian relations and wanted to experience the wilderness for herself. She joined Lisa on his next expedition to Fort Lisa, becoming the first white woman to travel up the Missouri River. It was on this trip that Lisa became ill and had to return to St. Louis. The couple returned to the city along with Mitain's daughter, Rosalie, and on the recommendation of a doctor, they moved to Sulphur Springs with the hopes that fresh air and mineral water would restore Lisa's health. Unfortunately, his health did not improve, and Manuel Lisa died on August 12, 1820, at the age of forty-eight.[44]

Despite Lisa's successes with Native American relations, he died with a substantial amount of debt. Mary decided that it was best to turn over management of the estate to her brother, Charles Hempstead, who quickly began to look for ways to pay down the debt. He first rented the Rock House to the U.S. Army for the storage of supplies that could be quickly loaded onto boats and transported to the forts along the Missouri River. Later, the warehouse was utilized by the Missouri Fur Company for storage of furs waiting to be sent east.[45]

Over the next few years, the property was sold multiple times and at one point became the storage warehouse for Lisa's former rival, the American Fur Company. Eventually, the Rock House was purchased by James Clemens Jr., cousin to Mark Twain, in 1828. It would remain in Clemens's ownership for

THE LEVEE AT ST. LOUIS, MISSOURI.—Photographed by R. Benecke, St. Louis.—[See Page 957.]

Wood engraving from *Harper's Weekly* showing steamboats along the levee in St. Louis, 1871. *Courtesy of the Missouri Historical Society, St. Louis.*

sixty years. Several businesses made their home in the Rock House, including Hicks, Ewing & Company's iron store (1836), John Clemens & Company sailmaker (1846), James Christy's Exchange Coffee House (1851–57), James Wilson's produce merchant (1852–73) and a saloon in 1880. The area of Wharf Street and Chestnut soon became known for its nickel whiskey, pig knuckles and fifteen-cent lofts.[46]

Between the 1880s and 1930s, the riverfront had an almost constant churn of boats, freight and people. With this came a unique new music fueled by the sound of the river, the pop of wagon wheels and the songs of workers as they hauled oversized loads up and down gangplanks. Work songs were commonplace along the levee and passed up and down the river as frequently as the boats would come and go. At the end of the day, these workers would take their meager wages and visit the nearby saloon, where the music continued. The songs shared along the river began to shape the music scene of St. Louis, making it the epicenter of ragtime music and eventually blues. W.C. Handy, the writer of the song "Saint Louis Blues," recalled being stranded, hungry and penniless as he slept on the cobblestones along the St. Louis levee. One night, he was standing outside a saloon full of white patrons when he felt himself being drawn in by the music. Being a Black man, he was treated rudely at first, but when the bartender learned that Handy could play the guitar and sing, he was invited to perform a few songs. After he collected his tips, Handy quickly left the saloon and purchased himself a clean change of clothes farther along Wharf Street. Places like the Rock House Saloon would eventually become a haven for musicians trying to get by and were an integral part of the St. Louis nightlife. Unfortunately, this area also became associated with crime as the mix of drink, poverty and a hard life led to many poor decisions. It was not uncommon to see the Rock House Saloon or at least the corner of Levee and Chestnut mentioned in the daily crime reports with such accusations as assault, robbery and murder.[47]

In 1900, the Old Rock House was more than eighty years old and starting to show its age. F.H. Ludington purchased the property, and according to local newspapers, he planned to demolish the building and replace it with a large warehouse for the Chase Bag Company. It is unknown why this didn't come to pass, but the Rock House Saloon continued a steady business. Unfortunately, this was just the beginning of the demolition conversations that would threaten the Old Rock House. In 1903, the Terminal Railway purchased the building and associated land as part of a project to build an elevated structure connecting the Eads Bridge to the Merchants' Terminal Railway. The project became controversial among property owners, who began to protest bills associated with the Terminal Railway extension. During a meeting of the City House of Delegates, one councilman remarked that the Terminal Association had "already violated existing franchises which it enjoys," and another was concerned that the tracks would cut off access to riverboats in the business part of the city.[48] Ultimately, a legal battle would ensue between St. Louis and the Terminal Railway, leaving the Old Rock House in limbo but saving it from destruction.

In 1928, the Terminal Railway began to rent the Old Rock House to Albina "Mom" Paintinda, and the building found new life. During Prohibition, the first floor held a restaurant, while the family lived on the second floor. They rented the third-floor rooms to levee workers. As time passed, the river trade slowed and, along with it, the lunch business. With the end of Prohibition, the family decided to move to the third floor and open a nightclub on the second. The entertainment featured African American performers and a regular vocalist who came to call herself "Rockhouse Annie." Other venues opened along the levee, and suburbanites would find their way down to the river's edge to enjoy a night of music and dancing.[49]

Around the same time, conversations began regarding the creation of a memorial park along the riverfront to celebrate the Louisiana Purchase

Men standing outside the Old Rock House Saloon, 1900–1904. *Photo from William Vincent Byars Courtesy of the Missouri Historical Society, St. Louis.*

and the pioneers of early St. Louis. The Jefferson National Expansion Memorial Association was formed in 1934, and the National Park Service opened an office in St. Louis in 1936. That same year, the National Park Service purchased all of the property along the riverfront, including the Old Rock House. Eviction notices soon followed, and businesses made plans to permanently close their doors. The Old Rock House continued to operate until the Paintinda family were forced to leave on October 15, 1939.[50]

The original plan was to demolish all of the buildings in this part of the city except the Old Courthouse, the Old Cathedral and the Old Rock House. Beyond that, there wasn't any design plan, and the city was to be left with a very large vacant lot, which caused frustration with the business owners pushed out of their livelihoods.[51] Nonetheless, demolition began around the Old Rock House.

Since the Old Rock House was to become a permanent fixture in the park, it was decided that it should be restored to its original 1800s condition. Before the restoration process could even begin, it was discovered that the many repairs done to the building over the years had destroyed much of the original structure, and what remained was not completely salvageable. Despite this hurdle, the project pushed forward with plans to re-create much of the structure utilizing methods from the period. Chestnut Street was closed on January 8, 1941, so restoration could begin, with workers having to be taught how to successfully replicate the former warehouse. The project was completed in February 1942.[52]

With no additional funds or plans for moving forward with the memorial park, the Old Rock House sat empty until the Coast Guard began using it to keep prisoners in August 1943. It used the space through 1945, when it requested to rent the third floor of the city jail as the Old Rock House was too small, had inadequate sanitary facilities and was not sufficiently secure. That same year, local organizations were finally able to initiate a campaign to finance the memorial park, and a competition was held to solicit designs. The committee selected a design by architect Eero Saarinen that included museums, forests, restaurants, a tea pavilion, a frontier village and all three buildings set to be preserved (Old Courthouse, Old Cathedral and Old Rock House). The Old Rock House appeared in his design as the entrance to the Gateway Arch, the centerpiece of the new park. Of course, having a design in hand did not move the project along, as problems were raised regarding the railroad lines that further delayed the project to 1956. While negotiating the railroad situation, the plans changed, and when it was all said and done, the Old Rock House was no longer on the map.[53]

The public quickly responded with frustration and anger. The city had developed a habit of dismantling historic buildings, and the citizens were getting tired of losing these connections to the past. To quell the anger, the National Park Service reassured the community that the Old Rock House would be rebuilt in another location. Appeased, citizens backed down from their complaints, and a contract was approved for the removal of the Old Rock House. With a plan to reconstruct the building at a later date, the stones needed to be numbered and kept along with the timbers and hardware before being placed in storage. In 1965, an article in the *Post-Dispatch* stated, "Most of the Old Rock House is missing and presumed to be lost." The story uncovered the fact that most of the building had not been saved. During the 1941 renovation, it was estimated that less than 20 percent of the original structure was utilized, and therefore when it was dismantled in 1959, only a small portion of the stones were saved. Those stones were stored in the basement of the Old Courthouse. The article ended with reassurances that once funds were available, a reconstruction of the Old Rock House would be erected at the south end of the park.[54]

Old Rock House photo from 1925–28. *Courtesy of the Missouri Historical Society, St. Louis.*

In 2018, the National Park Service finally removed the original stones from the basement of the Old Courthouse and began assembling a riverside façade of the Old Rock House in the Museum at the Gateway Arch.[55] This is in no way the reconstruction that the citizens were promised in the 1950s, but enough time had passed that many did not even notice. Today, visitors can enter a partial reproduction of the building and try to imagine what it would be like to experience St. Louis on the banks of the Mississippi in the 1800s.

You might be asking yourself: how can a building that no longer exists be haunted? Over the years, I have learned that any structure—given enough time to fill with laughter, song, anguish, triumph and the everyday routine of life—can create an imprint on an area. There are whispers of the riverfront being haunted by the sounds of the Old Rock House. People claim to hear the bluesy sound of a woman singing and the laughter of nightlife. Horse hooves can be heard clomping down a cobblestone street where now mostly cars pass. Along this part of the river, there are no clubs and no nightlife to be found, so where do these sounds come from? Did the energy of a once loved and spirited building soak into the limestone bedrock, and is it now nothing more than an echo of songs from the past?

CHAPTER 4

THE LEGEND OF STAGGER LEE

A s the daughter of a blues musician, I learned early on that stories take on a new life when accompanied by a soulful rhythm, and the story becomes as much a part of the listener as the writer. The history of St. Louis can be found not just in newspaper articles, books and old buildings but in the songs that accompany a person's day. With the steady stream of riverboat traffic along the levee, music was a consistent presence, as the workers rhythmically went about their day and the songs of every riverside city migrated to the shore. One song in particular resonated so deeply with the African American population of St. Louis that it morphed into a folk tale filled with warnings about drinking, guns and touching the wrong man's hat. There have been at least fifty songs recorded recounting the story of Stagger Lee, with the details of the story changing slightly with each telling suiting the needs of the time, the writer and the listener.

At the end of the Civil War, downtown St. Louis saw sweeping changes as formerly enslaved people moved north looking for work. As a riverboat port, St. Louis boasted opportunities for people willing to work the docks, railway and factories. In addition, the completion of the Eads Bridge in 1874 created a new way for people to travel from Illinois to Missouri. Between 1850 and 1900, the population of St. Louis increased sevenfold, reaching more than 500,000 by 1900, making it the fourth-largest city in the United States. As for the Black population, it grew by 21 percent between 1880 and 1890, with 85 percent of Black St. Louisans residing in 2 percent of the area.[56]

Broadway Street looking north toward Chestnut Street, 1891. *Courtesy of the Missouri Historical Society, St. Louis.*

The Chestnut Valley (around Market and Chestnut Streets) became a popular destination for both the Black and white population of the city. Anyone walking along these streets could easily find a good time, which included ragtime music, whiskey, gambling parlors and brothels. If one walked about five blocks north, they would notice incremental changes as they moved into the Deep Morgan (between Morgan/Convention Plaza and Biddle Streets). Also known as the "Bloody Third Ward," the Deep Morgan catered to Black society offering similar entertainments as the Chestnut Valley but also vaudeville theaters, blues music and billiard parlors.[57] This is where the legend of Stagger Lee began.

When researching news of the man known as Lee Shelton (Stagger Lee), it quickly becomes clear that by 1895 he was already a well-known character in the Deep Morgan. His exploits included being arrested for having brass knuckles (May 1884), loafing (November 1884), lounging (August 1885), assault and battery (November 1887), robbery (October 1888), assault with intent to kill Horace Jones (May 1889), assault with attempt to kill Dan

O'Leary (September 1890), passed out in an opium joint (September 1894), burglary (September 1890), robbery (February 1892), assault (November 1894) and firing a shot at another man (January 1895).[58] He was also on the receiving end of a few fights, including the day Charles Adams fired four shots at him (June 1887) and when Henry Massey beat him in the head with a brick (May 1889).[59] Shelton was no stranger to a fight, so it is unsurprising that prison records later describe him as having two scars on his right cheek, two scars on the back of his head and one scar on his left shoulder blade. Records further indicate that he was a mixed-race man with dark hair and eyes, stood five feet, seven inches tall and had a crossed left eye.[60]

Other than committing crime, what did Shelton do for a living? According to one newspaper, Lee Shelton was a carriage driver, and another named him the president of the Four Hundred Club (a Democratic social organization for young Black men that met at the Curtis Saloon). The legends tell that he was also a gambler, the proprietor of the Modern Horseshoe Club and a pimp associated with a group known as the "Macks" or "Macquerels."[61] If these legends are true, Shelton would have been able to utilize his job as a carriage driver to direct city visitors to his nightclub, the local bordellos and his girls in particular.

On the night of December 25, 1895, thirty-one-year-old levee hand William (Billy) Lyons and his friend Henry Crump were out for a night on the town. After leaving the Bridgewater Saloon, they walked a few blocks down the street to the Bill Curtis Saloon on the corner of Eleventh and Morgan Street. Billy, having had a few negative encounters in the bar previously, asked his friend to lend him a weapon just in case something was to happen. The Curtis had a reputation for crime, and more than one murder had occurred in and around the bar. So, Henry handed his friend a knife as they entered the building.[62]

Meanwhile, thirty-year-old Shelton strolled through the Deep Morgan looking for a way to entertain himself. As a "Mack," Shelton likely would have been seen wearing his finest Christmas attire, including a box-back coat, shiny St. Louis flats and his pristine white Stetson hat. Authors have further envisioned Shelton wearing bright colors and carrying a gold-tipped cane, with a series of gold rings adorning his fingers. If true, Shelton would have made quite the impression as he entered the Bill Curtis Saloon around eight o'clock that night. Standing in the doorway, he called out to the crowd "Who's treating?" and made his way to Billy.[63]

The pair were soon seen having a friendly conversation, occasionally laughing, as they enjoyed their drinks. By ten o'clock, they had both had too much whiskey, and the conversation had turned to politics. Billy was associated the Bridgewater Saloon, where the Republican meetings were held for that ward. On the other hand, Shelton was actively involved with the Democrats of the city. Political affiliations were shifting among the African American population in St. Louis due to promises they felt the Republicans had failed to keep. This shift made political conversations difficult even when sober, so it isn't surprising that the pair became increasingly agitated under the influence of drink. At one point, Shelton grabbed Billy's derby hat and broke the form. Billy became increasingly upset and told Shelton that he owed him "six bits" for the hat. He then grabbed Shelton's Stetson and held it out of reach. Shelton angrily asked for the return of his hat. The response was "No." Patrons of the bar later reported hearing Shelton calmly tell Billy, "If you don't give me my hat I'll blow your brains out."[64]

Billy was seen shoving his hand into his pocket to grab the knife Henry had given him several hours before. Whether or not the knife made it out of his pocket would become a point of argument later. What we do know is that Shelton pulled his .44 Smith & Wesson revolver from his coat and shot Lyons in the abdomen. He then walked over, took his hat and said, "I told you to give me my hat." He put the hat on his head and casually walked out of the bar. Billy was taken to the hospital and died of his wound at four o'clock in the morning December 26, 1895.[65]

Around 3:00 a.m., the police found Lee Shelton sleeping peacefully at the home of one of his girls on Sixth Street. He was arrested, and the woman of the house handed over the fully loaded .44 Smith & Wesson that Shelton had given her to store when he had arrived earlier. By Friday, December 27, Shelton had hired a lawyer (Nat Dryden) who was well known in Missouri as the first lawyer in the state to gain a conviction of a white man for murdering a Black man. That same day, an inquest was set at the coroner's office, where Shelton was met by a crowd of angry Black people hissing and cursing at him. Police had to draw their weapons to keep the crowd back, and Shelton was led into a room containing the body of Billy Lyons and several witnesses. Witness statements were taken, and Shelton was returned to jail.[66]

On June 25, 1896, a local pawnbroker, Morris H. Smit, paid Shelton's $3,000 bond (more than $100,000 today), and Shelton was able to enjoy a bit of freedom before his trial began. Jury selection began on July 13, and five days later, that jury was unable to agree on a verdict. The vote stood at seven for second-degree murder, two for manslaughter and three for acquittal. Dryden had argued that Shelton shot Billy in self-defense. The jury was dismissed, and a retrial was ordered. On August 26, 1896,

Crowd of people outside of the City Morgue at the corner of Spruce and Twelfth Streets, 1896. *Courtesy of the Missouri Historical Society, St. Louis.*

Shelton's lawyer, Nat Dryden, died after a night of drinking and was not able to represent Shelton in his retrial.[67]

The second trial began May 10, 1897, and Shelton was newly represented by former Missouri governor Charles P. Johnson. Henry Bridgwater was adamant that Shelton be punished for his crime and hired one of the best lawyers in St. Louis, C. Orrick Bishop, as the prosecuting attorney. On May 14, the *St. Louis Globe-Democrat* reported, "Lee Shelton Gets Twenty-Five Years" after the jury returned a verdict of guilty in the case. The judge granted Shelton an appeal on July 3, and a new bond was set at $7,500. While there is no record in the newspapers of the appeal trial, it clearly did not go in Shelton's favor, as he is listed among the thirteen prisoners being transferred to Missouri State Penitentiary on October 7, 1897.[68]

Shelton served just over twelve years before he was paroled by the governor on Thanksgiving Day 1909. He was free less than a year and a half before he was arrested for breaking into a man's home, beating him over the head with a revolver, breaking his skull and then stealing $140. Shelton was sent back to prison. Unfortunately, this time, he was sick with tuberculosis and rapidly began losing weight. His political friends pleaded with the governor to have mercy on Shelton and free him. The governor eventually agreed, but the Missouri Attorney General's Office objected to the parole leaving Shelton to die in prison on March 11, 1912.[69]

To this day, the story gets modified and retold through song, but what of the haunting? Well, Stagger Lee's home has been reported to be 911 North Twelfth Street (Tucker Boulevard) and is the last remaining building on that street from the 1890s. Upon further investigation, this wasn't Shelton's home, as he lived across the street at 914 North Twelfth Street. Despite this error, people have reported a suspicious man loitering outside the house who is on the shorter side, nicely dressed and with a bad eye. He soon vanishes without a trace.

Those who have stayed in the home have reported feelings of uneasiness, paranoia, hearing an angry male disembodied voice and lights that dance across walls, in windows and down the stairs. Likely the most frightening story comes from a house cleaner who was working on the upper floor. She could hear a man stumbling around in the kitchen. Unable to get past the man, she called the cops and locked herself in a room to await their arrival. Once there, the cops checked the entire building and found no one in the house other than the worker. You might ask why Shelton would stick around this house, but as the last remaining building from the era, it is likely familiar to him. Also, I have found in my investigations that using the name of someone in a location, even when they aren't associated with it, can cause strange things to happen. Nonetheless, one only needs to look around the city and note the wild nightlife and see that nothing much has changed, so why wouldn't Shelton be loitering on the corner? Perhaps staking out his next crime or waiting on a girl.

CHAPTER 5

THE CAMPBELL HOUSE

St. Louis has a few nicknames: "Mound City," "River City," "The Lou," "Rome of the West" and "Gateway to the West." It is this last one that the city takes pride in the most because it reflects why people came to reside in St. Louis. The city was founded in 1764 by French fur traders because, from this location, they could access the great wilderness to the west while also being able to transport their goods to the north, south and east. Many were enticed to St. Louis by the promise of western adventure and the potential for vast wealth. Among those who found themselves caught up in the allure of the American frontier was Robert Campbell.

Robert Campbell was born in Northern Ireland in 1804, and his father passed when Robert was only six years old. Robert and his three brothers each inherited a portion of their family's agricultural land and the responsibility of keeping their family afloat. While one may think that owning land would have put the Campbell brothers in a better position than most, it still left the family struggling to make ends meet. The Irish people were suffering from a variety of religious and political pressures that had led many to the brink of starvation. Knowing that the family could not continue to support everyone in the household, Robert's brother Hugh traveled to America to find work. Hugh quickly found a job as a store clerk in Milton, North Carolina, and began to send money back to Ireland to help support the family. Over the next three years, Hugh's regular financial support was accompanied by letters describing his experiences in America, and Robert began to imagine experiencing this New World for himself.[70]

In 1822, Robert decided that it was time for him to set out for America. He hoped to improve his financial situation and maybe find a little adventure along the way. In Philadelphia, Robert took a job as a clerk and began to learn about the American fur trade. It was here that John O'Fallon would offer Robert an assistant clerk position at his Bellevue post in what is today eastern Nebraska. Robert traveled out to the post and spent what was likely a cold winter learning what he could about fur trading in this part of the frontier while coping with a resurgence of his childhood breathing problems.[71]

In the spring of 1824, Robert was sent to work at O'Fallon's St. Louis store. While there, Robert met with a doctor, who advised him that the best way to restore his health would be to go to the Rocky Mountains, where he could find fresh air. Before he could decide his next course of action, Robert received word that his brother James had died in October of the previous year and that his sister, Elizabeth, had died in May 1824.[72] Saddened by the loss of his siblings and feeling pressured to return to Ireland, Robert weighed his options and decided that he had to stay the course in America, as it was his best chance to be able to support not just himself but his family.

Robert accepted a clerk position with an expedition heading for the Rocky Mountains in November 1825 and embarked on an adventure that would have him facing harsh weather, wild animals, rival traders and attacks by Native Americans. Four years later, he returned to St. Louis to sell the beaver pelts he had on hand and then ventured to Philadelphia to research prospects for going into business for himself. This was followed by a trip to see his brother, Hugh, and his new wife in Richmond, Virginia. Robert discussed forming a partnership with Hugh in which Robert would head west to collect pelts and Hugh would sell them in Philadelphia. Of course, these dreams would take a back seat as Robert was finally convinced to return to Ireland to help resolve ongoing financial issues. When he returned to St. Louis in June 1831, he formed a partnership with William Sublette and ventured back into the wilderness.[73]

From 1832 to 1835, Campbell and Sublette found some success by participating in the rendezvous trade but eventually turned their attention to building forts in an attempt to challenge the dominant American Fur Company. In September 1836, they purchased their first building on Main Street in St. Louis and opened a dry goods store. No longer making all of the trips themselves, Campbell and Sublette supplied goods to parties heading west and purchased furs from the traders when they returned. This involved long trips to the East to sell the furs they had purchased and procure supplies for the next round of expeditions. Campbell and Sublette would run their business mostly on loans and ultimately found themselves spending a substantial amount of time chasing down clients to pay their debts.[74]

In 1835, Robert was suffering from an illness that included fever, shivering and weakness that necessitated a change of scenery. He decided that it was best to leave the dirty streets of St. Louis and visit his brother Hugh so he could rest and recover. It was here that Robert met thirteen-year-old Virginia Kyle. As Hugh's sister-in-law, she regularly spent time at Hugh's home and helped care for Robert while he was ill. Over time, Robert fell in love with the vibrant young girl. His affections quickly met extreme disapproval from his family, her family and his partner, William Sublette. Robert was not one to be deterred and took to writing to Virginia regularly and sending her gifts when he could. When he asked for her hand in marriage in January 1838, she happily accepted. Unfortunately, her mother, Lucy Kyle, became a formidable barrier to the union. When Robert requested Lucy's blessing, she wrote back that she would not give away her child and explained how she hoped Virginia would finish school and choose a life of her own. Further, she stated that she would not consent for her daughter to marry under the age of eighteen.[75]

While disheartened by Lucy's response, Robert did not give up his goal of marrying Virginia. He wrote her regularly while maintaining his business in St. Louis. For the most part, she returned his sentiments but didn't hide the fact that she did not look forward to living in St. Louis. Six months after accepting Robert's proposal, Virginia changed her mind and told him that maybe eighteen was too young to marry. Robert was devastated but not deterred. He kept writing her letters pleading that she reconsider, and by June 1839, she told him that she wanted nothing more to do with him. Virginia then quit school and moved to Richmond, Virginia, to explore life without the pull of her mother or the constant pleadings from Robert.[76]

Virginia dated several men while in Richmond and even pondered at least one marriage proposal. After some time, her mother reconsidered Robert's proposal and began to write to Virginia about how marrying Robert Campbell would be a very good idea. He was clearly a well-respected and trustworthy man who cared deeply for Virginia. Meanwhile, Robert did his best to abide by Virginia's request not to write her, but in December 1840, he broke down and wrote her to express how much he missed her and hoped that she would reconsider marriage. Having now experienced two years of living life as she pleased, she agreed to marry Robert. Arrangements were quickly made, and thirty-seven-year-old Robert married nineteen-year-old Virginia on February 25, 1841, in Raleigh, North Carolina.[77]

The couple returned to St. Louis and took up residence in the Planter's House on Fourth Street. They celebrated the birth of their first child, James Alexander, on May 14, 1842. Virginia appeared to love being a mother and indulged James to the best of her ability. While Robert was away on his business trips, Virginia would take James on summer trips to visit family without a nurse, as she felt it only right that she be the one to care for her child despite what societal norms might have said at the time.[78]

Their second son, Hugh, was born on October 9, 1843, but sadly died of pneumonia four months later. Their third son, Robert, was born on November 27, 1844, and was quickly followed by the birth of their fourth child, Lucy Ann, on July 4, 1845. It was becoming increasingly apparent that the Campbells needed a home of their own. After living in the hotel for the first four years of their marriage, Robert purchased a house on the corner of Elm and Fifth Street (near current-day Busch Stadium), and the family happily moved in while Robert prepared for another purchasing trip east. Campbell and Sublette's business had been struggling under the weight of debtors, and William Sublette's health was starting to become a concern. He had been showing signs of tuberculosis despite taking time to rest at his Sulphur Springs plantation and resort. William Sublette's final business trip would be in the summer of 1845, and he died in a Pittsburgh hotel room. Despite his grief over losing his dear friend, Robert pushed on to finish the business the pair had set out to complete.[79]

Upon returning to St. Louis, Robert became increasingly involved in political issues, taking on the position of a state militia colonel and inspector general in 1846. Feeling that Native American relations were creating increasing problems for his trade business, he lobbied Washington to create an Indian agency to help settle disputes between the Native Americans and the European settlers. His efforts were ultimately successful, and he was able to get an old friend, Thomas Fitzpatrick, named as Indian agent. Soon after, he was named president of the Bank of Missouri, which allowed him to monitor the business conditions throughout the state and earned him greater respect in the community. During this time, he became increasingly aware of the power of the railroad to change the landscape of business and eventually decided to invest $10 million in the Pacific Railroad Company.[80]

While his business ventures were improving, things at home quickly deteriorated as two-year-old Robert died on July 2, 1847. This was quickly followed by the death of two-year-old, Lucy Ann, in September. Virginia was pregnant with Campbell's fifth child and likely felt anxious about the continued well-being of their family. They had already lost three children to illness and hoped that no more deaths would follow. St. Louis was an expanding city with ever-increasing amounts of pollution, and citizens were becoming concerned that this might be affecting their health. Despite an explosion in population, the city had neglected to invest in basic services such as sewage removal, clean water, garbage collection, firefighters and hospitals. St. Louis was quickly becoming a suitable habitat for disease. It is likely that Virginia became more vigilant in the care of the children and employed the assistance of the best doctors in St. Louis. On November 15, 1847, the Campbells celebrated the birth of their fifth child, Hugh (the second child with that name), and prayed that he and his only surviving sibling, James, would lead long lives.[81]

Unfortunately, the year 1849 would bring yet more tragedy to the Campbell family. It is estimated that one-tenth of the population of St. Louis (4,285 people) died of cholera that year, but historians caution that death records were not always accurate in pinpointing the exact cause of illness and it is possible that a much larger number of people died from the effects of cholera. Among those to lose their life to the fast-acting and painful disease was seven-year-old James Campbell. Hugh also became sick with the disease but thankfully survived. Having lost four children in the span of seven years likely put a strain on the family as they awaited the birth of their sixth child, Mary, in September.[82]

Cholera wasn't the only problem in St. Louis that year, and Robert Campbell experienced a different type of loss when a fire broke out on the steamboat *White Cloud* on May 17. The fire quickly spread up the wharf, alighting twenty-three additional steamboats, and then moved into the city, where it claimed fifteen square blocks and four hundred buildings, one of them being Campbell's store. Thankfully, his business was insured, and he was able to use the funds to pay off the remaining debts from Sublette and Campbell. He also sold the building lot and purchased a larger building down the street.[83]

Robert and Virginia Campbell would lose yet another child shortly after Christmas 1850. One-year-old Mary became seriously ill and suffered from swelling in her brain that ultimately led to her death. The Campbell family had experienced more loss than could be normally expected and began to look for any means to keep the little family they still had. Having become increasingly wealthy, Robert was able to send Virginia and their only remaining son, Hugh, away during the blistering summer months when filth and disease tended to flourish in St. Louis. They would visit Robert's brother in Philadelphia while Robert conducted business on the East Coast.[84]

During the summer of 1851, Robert had to leave his pregnant wife and only son to venture back into the frontier. He had been appointed to a committee tasked with negotiating the safe passage of European settlers west through tribal lands. That September, more than ten thousand Native Americans gathered for the signing of the Fort Laramie Treaty of 1851. In return for the tribes allowing safe passage for settlers, the U.S. government agreed to pay annuities to the tribes of $50,000 per year for the term of fifty years. With this work completed, Robert returned home and celebrated the birth of his seventh child, Robert (the second child with that name). Unfortunately, the family's joy was short-lived, as small Robert died of scarlet fever at the age of one.[85]

Engraving of Robert Campbell by Samuel Sartain. *Courtesy of the Missouri Historical Society, St. Louis.*

In 1854, Robert Campbell purchased a new home for his family, hoping to improve their overall health and well-being. The house at no. 20 Lucas Place was ten blocks away from the dangerous wharf section of town and in what was considered a very exclusive neighborhood. The Campbells were not the first to reside in the house, but Virginia was determined to put her mark on their new residence by lavishly furnishing the two-story home. Two years after moving into the house, Virginia's mother, Lucy, agreed to live with the family and help Virginia raise her children.[86]

Between 1853 and 1864, Virginia gave birth to six more children; Hazlett Kyle, Robert (the third child with that name), Hazlett Kyle (the second child with that name), James Alexander (the second child with that name), George Winston and John. The first of these children died of measles in November 1856 at the age of three. Young Robert died of diphtheria at the age of six in 1862. George Winston only lived five months, and John died from spina bifida at two weeks old in 1864. Of the thirteen children born to the Campbell family, only three survived past the age of eight. While the mortality rate for white children in the 1850s and 1860s was high at roughly 18–21 percent, the Campbell family experienced a substantially higher rate of 76.9 percent.[87]

While facing their ongoing personal tragedies, the Campbell family soon became concerned with the increasing tensions of a country divided. Robert Campbell considered himself a Constitutional Unionist and hoped that secession could be avoided. He supported the Crittenden Compromise, which would have enshrined slavery as a Constitutional right. Ultimately, the proposal was not supported by Congress, and the country became embroiled in a costly civil war. While Robert did support a state's right to allow citizens to own slaves, he no longer owned any himself. His last, Eliza, and her two sons, were freed in 1857 likely due to Virginia's increasing distaste for the institution. Virginia's mother, Lucy, had freed her enslaved laborers in 1842.[88]

After Robert's initial push for compromise, he stepped away from the political side of the war and instead focused on business by taking on contracts to supply the Union army with wagons, draft animals and various other supplies. In addition, he kept his eye on the affairs of the Native Americans. The Sioux had begun a revolt in August 1862, and war quickly spread across the northern plains. Despite the war, traders still needed to maintain their routes to supply trading posts and deliver annuities to friendly tribes. It was during these continued conflicts that Robert's eldest son, Hugh, asked to travel up the Platte River Valley to visit a friend. Having lost so many children, it is likely that Virginia was strongly opposed to this idea. Nonetheless, Robert agreed to let his son travel to Fort Laramie, where he later wrote to his parents about the excitement of shooting a gun and meeting a Native American boy Robert had assisted many years ago. To Virginia's relief, Hugh returned home safely at the end of the summer.[89]

By the end of the war, the Campbell family had acquired significantly more wealth and enjoyed a comfortable position in society despite some questions about Robert's loyalty to the Union. While opposed to the idea of a loyalty oath, Robert signed his in March 1863. With Robert now in his sixties, his business interests were primarily focused on finance, the railroad and real estate. In 1865, he built the Southern Hotel, which was noted to be "one of the most magnificent structures in the world, and the pride of the city."[90]

Meanwhile, the house at Lucas Place had grown with the family, and additions were added such as a carriage house, a third story and bay windows on all three stories of the east side. All three of the surviving children attended Smith Academy, which was located near the Campbell home. Hugh completed his Bachelor of Arts degree at Washington University in 1867, and after graduation, he began assisting his father with the family's enormous business interests and wealth.[91]

STATE OF MISSOURI,
COUNTY OF ST. LOUIS.

I, *Robert Campbell* do on oath declare that I have not at any time since the 17th day of December, A. D. 1861, wilfully taken up arms or levied war against the United States, nor against the Provisional Government of the State of Missouri, nor have wilfully adhered to the enemies of either, whether domestic or foreign, by giving aid and comfort or countenance thereto, but have always in good faith opposed the same; and further, that I will support, protect and defend the Constitution of the United States and of the State of Missouri against all enemies and opposers, whether domestic or foreign, and any ordinance, laws or resolutions of any State Convention or Legislature, or of any order or organization, secret or otherwise, to the contrary notwithstanding; and that I do this with an honest purpose, pledge and determination, faithfully to perform the same, without any mental reservation or evasion whatever, and that I will faithfully demean myself while in office.

Robert Campbell

Sworn to and subscribed before me, this *Thirty first* day of *March* in the year of our Lord eighteen hundred and *Sixty three*

Andrew Elliott

Notary Public

Loyalty oath signed by Robert Campbell in 1863. *Courtesy of the Missouri Historical Society, St. Louis.*

Hazlett and James were close enough in age that they attended school together, and both graduated in 1877. James went on to attend Yale University, where he studied law, while Hazlett took a clerk position with Brookmire and Rankin.[92]

In April 1877, a disastrous fire broke out in the basement of Robert Campbell's Southern Hotel. Due to the location of the fire, it quickly spread up the baggage elevator and engulfed the roof and upper floors in flames. The fire alarm was delayed, and the ten minutes lost trying to alert the fire department led to an unfortunate number of lost lives. Several people

The Southern Hotel after the fire, April 11, 1877. *Photo from Robert Benecke Courtesy of the Missouri Historical Society, St. Louis.*

jumped from the windows and died instantly. Others made ropes out of sheets in an attempt to climb out their hotel window but suffered serious injuries from the ultimate fall. After the smoke cleared, twenty-one people had lost their lives that day. Among the tragedy, there were moments of heroism, as the fire department was able to save sixteen servant girls from the sixth floor of the building by lashing together ladders that were not long enough to reach that height.[93]

Saddened by the tragedy, the citizens of the city responded by hosting fundraisers for the girls who had lost their jobs and for the families of the deceased. Celebrations were held to honor the firefighters, and Robert Campbell was asked if he would rebuild. Now in his seventies, Robert was at a point in his life where the stress of business was starting to show its signs on his health. The hotel was valued at $374,420 but was only insured for $282,420, leaving Robert at a loss. It's hard to know how heavy Robert's heart must have been with the loss of life associated with his hotel. With the support of the city, Robert did push forward to rebuild the Southern Hotel, but he would not live to see it resurrected from the ashes. His health had declined substantially, with his lung issues resurfacing. In an attempt to find relief, he took the family to the spas at Saratoga Springs in 1878 and 1879. While his health appeared to rally briefly, Robert died in his home on October 16, 1879, of a bronchial infection.[94]

As the eldest son, Hugh stepped in to assist his mother with the family finances and saw to the completion of the new Southern Hotel in 1881. The following year, Virginia died at the age of sixty, leaving the family's home and wealth to the three brothers. James returned from Yale after his mother's death and stayed in the home with his brothers until 1884, when they decided to tour Europe. While in Europe, Hugh took Hazlett to see a doctor, as he was concerned about his brother's deteriorating mental condition. In 1885, James went to Harvard to finish his education, while Hugh and Hazlett stayed in St. Louis. Hazlett had shown signs of mental illness early on in life, but after the death of his mother, these symptoms seemed to increase. Hugh had Hazlett examined by behavioral health specialists, but no help was received.[95]

Hugh spent the next few years caring for Hazlett. When James graduated from Harvard in 1888, Hugh likely saw an opportunity to take a break from being his brother's sole caretaker, and the brothers traveled to Paris. While there, James had a portrait commissioned of himself and his two dogs by the French painter Jules LeFebvre. Sadly, the brothers' stay ended abruptly when James became ill with influenza and died in 1890. Hugh had all of James's possessions returned to the Campbell home and his painting hung in the parlor. When writing his own will, he donated James's portrait to Yale University with the instructions to construct a building and name it in honor of James.[96]

As Hazlett's mental health continued to deteriorate, Hugh found himself becoming his brother's primary caretaker. Due to their closeness in age, James and Hazlett had been companions most of their life, and the loss of James was likely very difficult for Hazlett. He withdrew from the world and would often watch traffic from the upstairs windows of the house. Thankfully, Hugh had invested his family's wealth well, and the brothers were able to live without having to worry about money. Hugh never married or had children of his own, so he used his wealth to support Father Dunne's Newsboy's Home, where he often provided an annual Thanksgiving dinner to the boys. Hugh also hosted an annual Christmas dinner for his servants and their families at the Campbell house, allowing their children to take home their own ornaments.[97]

Unfortunately, the growing demands of Hazlett's care removed Hugh from society, and along with his brother, he became a recluse within the Campbell house. In 1924, Hazlett suffered a serious stroke that left him confined to his second-floor bedroom. Hugh did his best to care for his brother, but the long years of seclusion had to be wearing on him. Hugh died at the age of eighty-three in August 1931, leaving Hazlett as the last remaining member of the Campbell family. Hazlett was declared of "unsound mind" by doctors, and the estate was handled by lawyers. In March 1938, Hazlett died of pneumonia at the age of eighty.[98]

Hazlett's mental health caused problems even after his death, as there were several people who claimed to be heirs to his portion of the estate. Eventually, his estate was divided between descendants of his grandparents, and the heirs made the decision to auction the contents of the house. The house was donated to Yale as previously stipulated by Hugh, and the portrait of James was relegated to a storage unit at the university. As the last remaining house from Lucas Place, citizens became interested in preserving the house as a museum. The William Clark Society raised funds to purchase as many items as possible during the auction, and Stix, Baer and Fuller purchased the home from Yale University so it could be donated to the Campbell House Foundation.[99]

Using photographs of the house from the mid-1880s, the foundation restored the house to its original appearance, and the portrait of James with his dogs now hangs in the library.[100] Visitors to St. Louis can tour the house during regular business hours between the months of March and December.

In a house that experienced so much loss, it is not surprising to find a few ghostly stories. Volunteers and staffers have reported the sound of footsteps when the house is empty, and a guest said that she was lightly "nudged" while touring the home. On at least two occurrences, a museum volunteer ended his shift by closing the shutters, locking the doors and setting the security system only to return the next day to find the shutters in the third-floor library open and the fainting couch turned to face the windows. One of the quirkier incidents at the house is the appearance of half-dollar coins on the top step outside the building.[101] To date, no one has taken credit for this strange activity.

When a team member and I visited the home in 2021, we had several strange EMF (electromagnetic field) spikes near the portrait of James that could not be attributed to any known electrical device or outlet. We also experienced EMF activity associated with a small bear that we placed in the hallway leading into the children's rooms. By accident, we left the bear behind, and while it has been found on at least two occasions and placed somewhere safe for us to pick up, it quickly disappeared again without a

The Campbell House. *Author's collection.*

trace. My teammate and I agreed that the bear clearly needed to stay with the house. Are these odd occurrences caused by one of the Campbell children? Perhaps Hazlett is moving furniture around to get the best view from the library window. Is there a remnant of James in his beautiful painting? Is Hugh leaving coins behind as gifts to those who happen upon them? We may never know exactly who haunts the Campbell house, but it is possible that every family member occasionally visits their beautiful home at Lucas Place.

CHAPTER 6
BISSELL MANSION

Everyone loves a good haunted house story, with creaking doors and wispy white apparitions gliding down hallways. Of course, to have a ghost story, you have to have people who were attached to the property in some way. Learning about the people gives us perspective on why there may still be someone lingering in what appears to be an old and decaying building. In the case of the Lewis Bissell Mansion, it is very possible that the Bissell family found a place to be at peace and chose to never leave.

One paper called Lewis Bissell the "Son of Revolution." Born in 1789 in Manchester, Connecticut, he was the grandson of Captain Ozias Bissell, who served in the Revolutionary War. His father, Major Russell Bissell, also served in the Revolutionary War and the Indian Wars. Major Bissell was stationed at Fort Kaskaskia when the Lewis and Clark Expedition visited and was commandant of Fort Bellefontaine, where he died in 1807. Before knowing the fate of his father, nineteen-year-old Lewis Bissell was appointed as an ensign in the First Regiment, United States Infantry, and traveled to Fort Bellefontaine with his uncle, Colonel (later General) Daniel Bissell. Lewis Bissell remained at Fort Bellefontaine for only a few weeks before being sent to Fort Osage, where he would be assigned to garrison duty.[102]

At the start of the War of 1812, Lewis was ordered to the northern frontier, where he would fight in the Battle of Lundy's Lane near Niagara Falls. Despite being wounded in battle, Lewis persevered and earned the title of captain along with a post at Fort Bellefontaine. From here, he was given command of the gunboat *Governor Clark* and was assigned to patrol the

Missouri and Mississippi Rivers during the Portage des Sioux treaty meeting. It is estimated that between 1,500 and 2,000 warriors, women and children from more than a dozen tribes gathered for this historic event. Fur trader Manuel Lisa escorted forty-three Native American chiefs to the meeting, where William Clark was prepared to negotiate peace. After the treaty was signed, Captain Lewis Bissell was reassigned to command Fort Clark until his resignation in 1816.[103]

During his military career, Lewis Bissell must have been introduced to and ultimately recruited by John O'Fallon to work in the fur trade business selling provisions to the army. Bissell soon found himself a member of the Yellowstone Expedition up the Missouri River. The goals of the expedition were to expand and protect the fur trade while also establishing control over the Native American tribes of that area without invoking hostility. The expedition reached Council Bluffs in September 1819 and stopped to set up camp. Unfortunately, it was an extremely harsh winter, and the expedition was unprepared. With insufficient supplies to sustain the men, more than two hundred soldiers died from an outbreak of scurvy. That spring, the soldiers built a camp at Council Bluff and renamed it Fort Atkinson. Bissell remained here until 1822, when he left the fort in search of better air and a means to improve his health. He eventually ended up back in Connecticut, where he married Mary Ann Woodbridge and became a merchant. That same year, 1824, Bissell purchased 677 acres outside St. Louis. While their new home was being built, Lewis and Mary Ann remained in Connecticut. Their first child, James, was born in 1827, and their second child, Mary, was born in 1828.[104]

Having served in the military and traveled the Mississippi, Lewis Bissell wanted to settle down to a quiet life. He built his mansion atop a hill facing the Mississippi River, where he would be able to see far into the Illinois countryside. He would have plenty of land to farm and a beautiful home in which to raise his family. The mansion was one of the first built of brick in the St. Louis area and was arranged with four large rooms on each floor divided by a central stairway. The home provided ample room for the growing family, and they soon filled the space with the laughter of children. Their third child, George, was born in 1830, the same year that the family returned to St. Louis, and their fourth child, Anna, would arrive two years later.[105]

Sadly, Mary Ann passed away in 1834 at the age of twenty-seven, leaving Lewis alone in the mansion with four children to raise. It is unknown if Lewis mourned for Mary Ann longer than was traditionally expected for men of this era (typically six months) or if it just took him longer to find a suitable partner to help him raise his children. Nonetheless, Lewis did remarry almost four years later to Mary Jane Douglass. Between 1838 and 1855, the couple would have six more children: Cornelia, Lewis, Sophie, Eloise, Taylor and Harriet. With so many children, it is not surprising that the census records show that the Bissell family had six enslaved African Americans between 1840 and 1850. While their names are not recorded, the census shows a sixty-year-old man; three women aged forty-five, twenty-eight and twenty-six; a four-year-old girl; and an eight-year-old boy.[106]

On November 1, 1855, Lewis Bissell was among the six hundred passengers aboard the first Pacific Railroad train leaving St. Louis bound for Jefferson City. There had been questions about the safety of the track, but everyone had been reassured that all was well. While the bridge over the Gasconade River had not been completed, its builders had bolstered it with a temporary trestle that they expected would be sufficient for the first run of the train. With music and speeches, citizens celebrated the transcontinental railroad's presence in the city, and at 9:00 a.m. the locomotive *Missouri* departed the station with fourteen cars. At 1:30 p.m., the train moved onto the bridge, and the trestle quickly collapsed, sending the locomotive thirty feet into the mud. Thirty-one people died that day, and seventy others were seriously injured. Lewis luckily was in the last railroad car and escaped with only injuries.[107]

Captain Lewis Bissell spent the rest of his life quietly enjoying his family and his home. He rarely made the papers and likely preferred it that way. At the age of seventy-nine, Lewis Bissell died at home on November 25, 1868. With most of their children raised, Mary Jane decided to move to Virginia and left the house vacant. Five years later, she sold the mansion to her daughter Cornelia Provines and her husband, Alexander. Alexander was a wine merchant and eventually found it prudent to relocate to Healdsburg, California, in the heart of modern-day Sonoma Wine country. The Provines only lived in the Bissell mansion for four years and chose to rent out the family home for the next five years.[108]

In 1882, the house was sold to a butcher from Sturgeon Market, Frederick Kraft. He and his wife, Margaretha, purchased an additional lot to expand the property and added rooms to the west side of the mansion to accommodate their eight children. Frederick died in 1914, and the family members transferred the house to the sixth child, thirty-three-year-old Adele Kraft in 1916. Adele used the property primarily as a rental until 1925, when she sold it to Dr. Marie Randall and her husband, Edward Randall. Dr. Randall requested that the board of aldermen change the

THE PACIFIC

RAILROAD CELEBRATION.

The Citizens of Jefferson City and vicinity, respectfully invite you to visit this City, to participate with them in Celebrating the Opening of the Pacific Railroad to this point, which, it is expected, will take place on the First day of November proximo.

E. B. CORDELL,
JAS. L. MINOR,
THOS. L. PRICE,
C. J. CORWIN,
JAS. LUSK,
W. D. KERR,
J. B. GARDENHIRE,

R. W. WELLS,
R. A. WELLS,
B. BRUNS,
E. L. EDWARDS,
JNO. M. RICHARDSON,
A. W. MORRISON.

JEFFERSON CITY, October 17, 1855.

Invitation to the opening of the Pacific Railroad to Jefferson City, October 17, 1855. *Courtesy of the Missouri Historical Society, St. Louis.*

name of the street to Randall Place, and the mansion now officially sits at 4426 Randall Place.[109]

The mansion was sold again in 1956 to the Graves family, who subdivided the home into nine apartments. Unfortunately, they were only in residence for two years before the Missouri Highway Commission announced plans to demolish the old mansion to make way for the Mark Twain Expressway

(Interstate 70). After receiving multiple complaints from the owners, citizens and the American Institute of Architects, the highway commission said it would explore options for moving the building only if the cost of moving the house fell within the commission's budget for the project. This is only one of the many historical buildings that had been threatened by the expansion of the city. Citizens interested in retaining historical properties had already lost the fight to save the Old Rock House, and within three years, the Lemp Mansion and the Chatillon-DeMenil Mansion would face similar fights with the Missouri Highway Commission.[110]

The Graves family lost their first legal battle with the highway commission and soon recruited the assistance of experts from the Missouri Historical Society, the City Art Museum and Washington University's School of Architecture. Due to the slope of the hill on which the Bissell Mansion sat, the highway engineers were certain that they needed to reconfigure the entire slope to reduce the potential for landslides onto the highway. Engineer Frank Hilliker argued that the problem could be solved by building a retaining wall instead. At first, the highway commission turned down this option, stating that it would be too costly, but Hilliker obtained cost estimates that not only proved his plan was more cost effective but also that it would save the mansion. The highway commission eventually relented, and a retaining wall was added to the construction plan.[111]

Despite being saved from the highway, Bissell Mansion would soon face the decline of the neighborhood. The old stately houses of Randall Place began to deteriorate and fall vacant. Urban blight was pushing citizens out of the area and into the western suburbs. As a boy, Stan Schepker would ride his bike past the Bissell Mansion and grew to love the beautiful old home. Seeing the property vacant and deteriorating prompted Stan to action, and he recruited his brothers along with three other area residents to form the Grand Bissell Towers Corporation. The corporation purchased the mansion in 1976 and received assistance from the Mercantile Bank, Small Business Administration and the Landmarks Association to renovate the building into a restaurant. The grand opening was a Mardi Gras party held in 1978.[112]

The restaurant was open for more than forty years and was well known for its murder mystery dinner theater. Sadly, the Schepker family closed the restaurant at the beginning of the COVID-19 pandemic in 2020, and the building sat vacant as the Grand Bissell Towers Corporation tried to determine the next best action. While Randall Place was still lined with large, beautiful homes with caring owners, the nearby community had further deteriorated. Fewer people were visiting the north St. Louis neighborhood,

The Bissell Mansion. *Author's collection.*

and the Schepkers were ready to retire. The mansion went up for sale in 2022 for $250,000. While vacant, thieves raided the home for copper. There was no air conditioning, the plumbing and electricity needed to be replaced and there was a hole in the roof allowing animals to come into the building.[113] The home has been taken off the market twice as of this writing, and the price was reduced to $225,000 in May 2024. Sadly, the future of the beautiful old mansion is unknown.

Will the reported hauntings impact the decision of a future owner to purchase the home? Over the years, employees of the Bissell Mansion Restaurant reported strange incidents in and around the house. Bartenders noted that wine glasses would go missing and then suddenly reappear in odd places. Others claimed to have seen a woman in white who wanders around the home, possibly one of Lewis Bissell's wives checking on her children. And then there is the man who stands in the parking lot looking admiringly up at the mansion. Is this Captain Bissell checking on his home? Is he impressed by the longevity of the mansion that has stood for more than 190 years? One can only hope that as spirits we can choose to return to the places we cherished in life, just to check in and see how long our legacy stands. In the case of Bissell Mansion, I hope the spirits soon see their home once again filled with joy.

CHAPTER 7
CITY HOSPITAL

How many hospitals does one city need? Within the current St. Louis City limits, there are eight distinct hospitals. If you expand the search into St. Louis County, another seven or eight can be found, more if you count the extensions to hospitals that have multiple locations. How did this happen? While it took some time for the city to establish its first hospital, over the years different populations of people decided that they needed their own hospital, so there came to be Catholic, Jewish, Protestant, Black, white, rich, poor and children's hospitals. It's fascinating to consider how a city went from not having the funds to build one hospital to becoming a hub for medical professionals.

St. Louis City was incorporated in 1822, and it elected its first mayor, William Carr Lane, shortly thereafter. Lane was a physician who had traveled from Philadelphia in 1819 to make his home in the growing city. During his inaugural address, Lane observed that it would be prudent for the city to look toward improvements that would benefit public health, which included the construction of a hospital to care for the sick.[114] Of course, St. Louis was not exactly a wealthy city and hardly had funds to consider paving the streets or effectively moving sewage away from populated areas. How could it ever consider such a luxury as a hospital?

Taking matters into his own hands, a wealthy merchant and real estate investor, John Mullanphy, made arrangements with Father Joseph Rosati to establish a hospital. Father Rosati was confident that the Sisters of Charity of St. Vincent DePaul would be able to staff the hospital, and Mullanphy agreed to donate the space, provide $150 for the Sisters' journey to St. Louis and give the Sisters an additional $350 to furnish the hospital when they arrived.[115]

Sisters Francis Xavier Love, Martina Butcher, Rebecca Dellone and Francis Regis Barrett were selected for the task and left Emmitsburg, Maryland, on the morning of October 15, 1828. During the twenty-one-day journey, the Sisters crossed 1,500 miles and experienced a frontier world they had never imagined. The Sisters accepted their first patients into the three-room log cabin turned hospital on November 26, 1828. It took little time for them to outgrow the small cabin, and by February 1832, John Mullanphy once again stepped in to provide a larger space for the necessary work. They expanded just in time, as the city was struck by a wave of cholera that same October. Soon after, their little hospital was designated the official city hospital and began to receive support from the city until a municipal facility could be opened in 1846.[116]

Cholera became a regular issue for the overpopulated and increasingly dirty city. In addition, the citizens suffered from various accidents and illnesses that come along with life on the river. In July 1845, the city council finally passed an ordinance authorizing the purchase of land for the construction of the new hospital. Nestled in what was the common fields along St. Ange Street, the ninety-bed hospital facility opened its doors to patients in 1846. Hospital admissions for the 1847–48 fiscal year totaled 1,214. Its location, just outside the more populated area, would be advantageous during the cholera epidemic of 1849, as it kept the hospital staff from contracting

Steel engraving of the City Hospital, 1854. *Created by August Gast & Company, courtesy of the Missouri Historical Society, St. Louis.*

the miserable disease and allowed them to work through the worst of the crisis. It is estimated that 10 percent of the population of St. Louis died of cholera that year, and a healthy medical staff helped keep the number from increasing further.[117]

In 1855, the city began to discuss moving the City Graveyard at the corner of St. Ange and Park Streets, adjacent to the hospital. The graveyard was quickly becoming overfull, and the city believed the ground could serve other, more lucrative purposes. The city began looking into a larger plot outside the city limits and made plans to relocate the bodies.[118]

Tragedy struck the hospital in May 1856 when a fire broke out in a lecture room located in the southwest wing of the hospital, quickly engulfing the entire building in flames. Dr. Bannister, the resident physician, and the superintendent, Mr. Roberts, rushed to evacuate the psychiatric patients, who were locked in their rooms. Next, they evacuated the sick who were unable to walk on their own, and the remainder of the patients were escorted out as quickly as possible. The only death reported was that of a psychiatric patient who ran back into the burning building. The surviving patients were taken to the Sisters of Charity Hospital to continue their care and treat any injuries sustained during the evacuation. They were later relocated to the Marine Hospital and the County Farm as a new building was constructed on the same site and reopened in July 1857.[119]

In February 1858, a resolution was adopted at the city board of delegates to "stop the exhumation of the remains of deceased persons interred in the old City Cemetery, on the corner of St. Ange and Park Avenues."[120] The reason for this is not clear, and whether the bodies were eventually moved remains a question. While this may seem not directly related to the hospital, it does eventually become a potential factor in the later claims of hauntings.

The hospital was able to carry on without too much controversy for almost forty years, but sadly things took a turn on May 27, 1896, when a deadly tornado demolished the building. Despite being in the direct path of the storm, only 2 patients died, but more than 100 were severely wounded. Patients were quickly moved from the upper stories of the hospital, and cots were set up on the lower floors. The kitchens, dining rooms and offices were utilized as triage rooms as the staff worked to treat the injured as quickly as possible. Those with the worst injuries were transported to the House of the Good Shepherd, while 150 patients were sent to the Alexian Brothers Hospital. One patient recounted how the extreme winds of the storm lifted him from his bed on the second floor and blew him into the yard below, where he quickly managed to retreat to the safety of the hospital basement.[121]

Evacuations from City Hospital after the tornado, May 27, 1896. *Photo from J.C. Strauss Courtesy of the Missouri Historical Society, St. Louis.*

Needing to rebuild the hospital yet again, the city had a vacant convent building repurposed for the hospital to use temporarily. Four years later, the *St. Louis Post-Dispatch* ran an article, "City Hospital Building Loses Sections of Plaster and Fast Falling to Pieces," highlighting the unsafe conditions patients were dealing with at the temporary facility. One evening, a ten-foot section of plaster fell from the ceiling and landed on a vacant patient cot. The next day, a loud rumbling sound was heard from the reception desk followed by a crash signaling the loss of a fifteen-by-ten-foot section of plaster that had collapsed on the staircase leading to the first floor.[122] Despite the rapidly deteriorating condition of the temporary hospital, it would take another five years for the new City Hospital to open its doors.

On August 10, 1905, 360 patients were moved from the temporary hospital to the new facility. Six ambulances, two omnibuses and three streetcars were used to safely transport the patients to the new building. The new facility consisted of eight buildings connected by a closed corridor, and it is likely that this is when the hospital began to utilize the grounds of the former City Graveyard.[123]

In 1909, the construction of a new administration and ward building facing Lafayette Street began, and the hospital soon became the center of the city's public health system. A Hospital Commission was established, and a hospital commissioner was elected to oversee the multiple medical facilities now serving the city. Facilities like the City Sanitarium, City Infirmary, the Robert Koch Hospital for Tuberculosis, the Isolation Hospital and the Snodgrass Laboratory of Pathology and Bacteriology would all fall under the administration of the commission. With the advancements in medical science, the hospital was able to begin utilizing X-rays, urinalysis and a bacteriological lab, making it easier to diagnose illnesses such as diphtheria, cholera, tuberculosis, malaria and other diseases. While the hospital had grown in its ability to admit and treat citizens, it was still not sufficient to care for all those in need. During the fiscal year 1912–13, the hospital had a total of 14,835 admissions.[124] Discussions for building a second hospital soon began.

The next major medical crisis to hit St. Louis was the influenza epidemic of 1918. In late September of that year, the St. Louis city health commissioner had been watching the spread of influenza from Boston westward and began to make plans for how to best shield St. Louisans from the worst of the effects. Physicians were advised to report any appearance of the illness in their patients, and citizens were instructed that the best

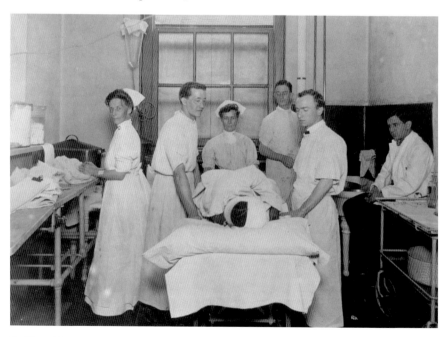

Staff working in the emergency room at St. Louis City Hospital, 1905. *Courtesy of the Missouri Historical Society, St. Louis.*

way to stay healthy was to avoid fatigue, alcohol, crowds and anyone who showed symptoms of being sick.[125]

On October 4, 500 cases of influenza were reported at Jefferson Barracks, and that night the first 7 cases were confirmed within the city limits. The board of alderman soon approved a bill stating that physicians would be fined for not reporting cases of influenza. In addition, the bill gave the mayor the authority to proclaim a public health emergency, which would give the health commissioner the authority to close businesses to prevent the spread of the illness. The closings began on October 8 with theaters, churches and public gatherings. The following day, schools were closed. By October 11, private hospitals had begun refusing influenza patients, City Hospital was at capacity and the Isolation Hospital had to be used to accept overflow cases. Four

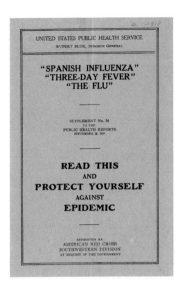

Informational pamphlet given to citizens with tips for protection against the "Spanish influenza," 1918. *Courtesy of the Missouri Historical Society, St. Louis.*

days later, the number of cases in the city was over 3,000, and by October 21, 6,005 people were reported to have contracted influenza, with 193 having died from pneumonia. On November 9, all non-essential businesses were closed throughout the city, with a total number of cases hitting 12,652 and 629 deaths from pneumonia. It wasn't until December 28 that the restrictions would be removed as the number of daily cases had fallen drastically. By spring, flu-related deaths in St. Louis City totaled 1,703, which gave the city one of the lowest death rates from influenza of any major city.[126]

What may be surprising to individuals living today is that the City Hospital provided treatment for free. Because of this, it was often crowded with impoverished citizens who had nowhere else to go for treatment. In an attempt to reduce the burden on the facility, the city opened City Hospital no. 2, leading to a segregated system for providing healthcare to citizens. The original hospital (now referred to as City Hospital no. 1) treated the white population, and City Hospital no. 2 was designated for Black St. Louisans. It quickly became apparent that the new hospital lacked many of the services available at the original hospital, and a new North St. Louis site was proposed. Homer G. Phillips Hospital opened in 1937.[127]

Despite the opening of a new hospital, City Hospital no. 1 continued to struggle with space issues. World War I intensified these problems as the government took over two of the campus buildings, creating an overflow in the remaining buildings. In addition, war efforts led to a serious staff shortage. Eventually, a new clinic building was opened in 1921 to ease the capacity issues. A few years later, the city approved an ordinance allowing City Hospital (nos. 1 and 2) to charge for services when patients could afford to pay. This didn't help the hospital when the Depression hit, and poor citizens still had nowhere else to go so they tended to fill the hospital to capacity. Between 1933 and 1934, a report noted that to treat newly sick patients, the hospital would have to discharge current patients before they were well enough to leave.[128]

In 1940, City Hospital no. 1 opened a remodeled clinic, a new laundry facility and a twelve-story hospital building. The new facilities increased the hospital capacity to 1,104 beds. With the space issues rectified, the hospital was once again facing staffing issues with a nurse's shortage in 1939 quickly followed by the start of World War II. The hospital pushed forward despite these difficulties and celebrated the opening of a state-of-the-art pathology lab in 1959. Unfortunately, the physician brought in to run the facility resigned after three years, citing low pay and an inability to retain staff. Further improvements were made in 1971, but the hospital was facing reduced patient counts.[129]

One major issue was the hospital's struggle to qualify for Medicaid assistance. Despite having desegregated the two hospitals, staff between the facilities were still largely split along color lines, which made the hospital system ineligible for funds. Recognizing that the city could no longer sustain two hospitals, Homer G. Phillips (City Hospital no. 2) was closed in 1979, and the two hospitals were consolidated back into City Hospital no. 1.

Unfortunately, this did not solve the problem, and by 1983, the hospital was averaging fewer than 250 patients a day and needed repairs that would cost upward of $40 million. City Hospital, which had grown from a small ninety-bed facility to a thirteen-building complex that covered four city blocks, closed in 1985. The hospital would face calls for its demolition over the next fifteen years, with several of the inner-campus buildings meeting the wrecking ball. Thankfully, the remaining buildings were saved in 2001 by being added to the National Register of Historic Places. In 2006, the hospital administration building opened with 102 loft condominiums.[130] The remaining buildings were eventually renovated as apartments.

Today, the old hospital is full of life once again. Of course, some have said that they could never live in a building where so many had died. Hospitals are

City Hospital has been converted into condominiums and apartments. *Author's collection.*

often associated with hauntings for this very reason, and I have investigated a few myself. Add a relocated cemetery to the mix and you have a recipe for paranormal phenomena. It is not uncommon in hospital hauntings to hear people report the sound of footsteps in hallways, the sound of doors opening and the occasional nurse checking in on a "patient."

I have a good friend renting an apartment in the building, and she says that she has heard a woman screaming in the hallway multiple times. She went out to make sure no one was hurt but found no one there. There is also a report that a few girls were checking out the buildings while it was still under renovation and suddenly were startled to hear a woman scream. As expected, they ran out of there as quickly as possible. Of course, narrowing down who haunts the City Hospital is near impossible considering the multiple deaths that would have occurred on site, along with the fact that untold numbers of people devoted their lives to healing the ill in that very space. It is very possible that former nurses, doctors and patients pass through the buildings on occasion and suddenly become confused because the hospital they once knew is now completely different. It is also possible that the daily movement of people through the building over the years imprinted on the space, creating a residual haunting that has no awareness of the laptops, televisions, treadmills and a million other "strange" items now filling their space.

CHAPTER 8

JAMES EADS AND HIS BRIDGE

*One who knows the Mississippi will promptly aver—not aloud, but to himself—
that ten thousand River Commissions, with the mines of the world at their back,
cannot tame that lawless stream, cannot curb it or confine it, cannot say to it,
Go here, or Go there, and make it obey; cannot save a shore which it has
sentenced; cannot bar its path with an obstruction which it will not tear down,
dance over, and laugh at.*
—Mark Twain

Those of us who live along the Mississippi River understand its power
and how it has shaped many lives by its existence. As someone who
has lost a home to the river's changing shores, I understand just
how terribly powerful a river can be. Despite the challenge, the river has
always attracted people to it and created great opportunities for those who
are willing to settle along its banks. St. Louis would not have become the
bustling city of the late 1800s and early 1900s without the mammoth river
connecting New Orleans to the center of the United States. And while Mark
Twain may have believed it impossible for any man to tame the river, one
man tried and won a few battles along the way.

At the age of thirteen, James Eads traveled to St. Louis with his mom
and two sisters on the steamboat *Belle West*. An inquisitive young boy,
James regularly questioned the boat pilot about the nuances of the river, its
navigation and how steamboats push against the current. It would be here
that James would develop a passion for the mighty Mississippi and learn

his first lessons about the dangers of river travel. Shortly before arriving at St. Louis, a fire broke out on the lower deck of the boat, destroying the family's belongings stored within. So, James and his family arrived in St. Louis with nothing but the clothes on their back. Despite this hurdle, they made the best of it and were offered a temporary place to stay while they tried to get themselves settled. James quickly found a way to make money by selling apples from a basket he carried around town, and his mom found a place to rent where she could prepare meals for local businessmen. As James wandered around town, selling his apples, he took breaks along the levee to watch the steamboats and dream of the day when he would build one of his own.[131] His family could not afford to send him to school, but that didn't matter to a determined James Eads. He knew he would figure it out.

James eventually gained a job working as an errand boy for Williams & Duhring dry goods store. In observing the boy, the owner saw a spark of intelligence that he thought best to foster, so he offered James the use of his personal library above the store. This library was filled with books on science, literature and history. Here James would spend his free hours learning everything he could about the world and how to build his steamboat. By 1839, nineteen-year-old James Eads had successfully built a six-foot steamboat and launched it on Chouteau's pond. He would go on to become the second clerk for the *Knickerbocker* steamboat and further his field education in all things river life.[132]

In 1842, James decided to try his hand at salvaging the valuable cargo from sunken ships that were lying on the muddy river bottom. While many had tried, scavenging the Mississippi River proved to be challenging due to the lack of visibility, unpredictable currents and thick layers of sand and mud. Never deterred by a challenge, James created a diving bell that looked like nothing more than a whiskey barrel with lead bars fastened to the bottom. He partnered with shipbuilders Calvin Case and William Nelson and took his first commission shortly thereafter. The first diver to view the contraption refused to go down in it and told James that he would like to be able to go home to his family at the end of the day, not end up as more debris at the bottom of the river. James reassured him that it would work and jumped into the diving bell himself. He traveled to the bottom of the river, where he recovered ten lead bars. Reassured, the diver agreed to use the bell. James's design would earn him and his partners a substantial amount of money over the next ten years. He eventually expanded his design, and by the 1850s, James was able to lift entire boats from the riverbed.[133]

Back home, James's wife, Martha, died from cholera in 1852, and his two daughters spent much of their time in the home of James's sister-in-law while James was away at work. Less than two years later, he married Eunice, the widow of his first cousin, and moved his family into a brick home at Fifth and Myrtle Streets. The family only lived here for a short period before James received the unfortunate news that the long hours at the bottom of the river had strained his heart. His doctor urged him to retire, and at the age of thirty-seven, James set aside his work on the river and purchased his Compton Hill mansion in south St. Louis. Here he enjoyed his library, gardens and spending time with his daughters, but James struggled to let go of the river.[134] Meanwhile, the country was changing, and political unrest was showing signs of turning violent.

As the Civil War erupted around him, James began thinking about how best to protect Union interests along the river. He had an idea for an armored gunboat and began speaking with friends and colleagues about his desire to build boats for the Union army. When the idea came to the secretary of the navy, he brushed it off saying that ironclad warships on the river were impossible and impractical. James didn't let this stop him and continued to argue his point to anyone who would listen. By the end of 1861, James Eads had a contract to build seven ironclad ships for the navy in sixty-five days. The secretary of the navy expected that James could not fulfill the contract in the amount of time specified and continued to pursue other avenues for maintaining the safety of the river. Of course, it was never wise to expect failure from James Eads. While he was unable to build his ships in sixty-five days, he nonetheless delivered the fleet another thirty-five days later. The ships allowed the Union army to take Vicksburg, Mississippi, and win battles at Fort Henry and Fort Donelson, creating safe passage along the Mississippi for the Union to transport troops and supplies.[135]

Shortly after the war, Eads turned his mind toward further improvements in navigating the Mississippi. He spoke often of asking the government to assist with clearing the river of debris that caused countless issues for the riverboats supplying the Midwest. His requests were often ignored, and he would eventually have to set his salvage ideas aside when presented with a new project for conquering the river.[136]

In February 1865, an act to incorporate the St. Louis and Illinois Bridge Company was passed by the Missouri legislature and was further amended in 1866 to include specifications for what type of bridge could be built. When the bill was approved, stipulations were added that made many feel the location of the bridge was impossible. The bill limited the bridge landing

Portrait of James B. Eads,
taken between 1861 and 1865.
*Courtesy of the Missouri Historical
Society, St. Louis.*

on the Illinois side of the river to within one hundred feet on either side of the dike in East St. Louis. This would require the Missouri side of the bridge to land in the heart of downtown St. Louis, on Washington Avenue. In addition, the St. Louis Union Merchants' Exchange added additional stipulations to ensure that river traffic could continue unimpeded. In an April 1866 meeting, it resolved that the bridge could not have a drawbridge and had to be constructed with continuous spans, one of which had to be at least five hundred feet in length. Further, the minimum clearance had to be fifty feet between the lowest portion of the bridge and the high-water mark, measured at the center of the greatest span.[137] These very specific requirements had many scratching their head and looking to amend the bill.

Believing that the project was essential for the city, James took the specifications as written and started drafting ideas for a bridge that would do what everyone thought was impossible. Meanwhile, several attempts were made to amend the bill and repeal the location restriction, but none was successful until L.B. Boomer pushed an amended bill through the

Illinois Senate in 1867. This bill removed the names of two of the former incorporators and set in motion a series of newspaper reports noting that Chicago businessmen were trying to gain exclusive rights to build the bridge and sell out St. Louis investors.[138]

During a meeting of the Union Merchants' Exchange in St. Louis on Saturday, February 16, 1867, it was argued that the new stipulations giving the corporation twenty-five years of exclusive rights to build could lead to companies opposed to the bridge owning a vast majority of the stock and delaying the project for years. The group decided that a committee would visit Springfield to request an amendment requiring investors to be sought first in St. Louis and that at least $500,000 be spent on construction within the first two years of stock sales. While this plan could have worked to keep interests in St. Louis, James had already drafted plans for a bridge that met all of the requirements of the original Missouri bill. He argued that since they had the approval to build that bridge, they just needed to reorganize the company and start building. Later that evening, the Missouri Senate received a bill to suspend the rule requiring ten or more people to incorporate for the purpose of building bridges, allowing for the approval of the St. Louis and Illinois Bridge Company to build a bridge over the Mississippi with James Eads as the chief engineer.[139]

Of course, this set in motion lawsuits attempting to determine which company had the rights to build a bridge at St. Louis—the Illinois and St. Louis Bridge Company, led by L.B. Boomer, or the St. Louis and Illinois Bridge Company, led by James B. Eads. On July 18, the *Daily Missouri Republican* printed an advertisement for 100,000 cubic yards of stone wanted for the bridge at St. Louis to commence by the start of September. Clearly, James was not waiting on lawyers to decide if St. Louis could build its bridge. On July 31, the St. Louis company made a formal request to the mayor to occupy the levee between Washington Avenue and Greer Street so as to begin construction of the first abutment, and detailed plans for the bridge were published in the paper on Sunday, August 4. By September 30, the first foundational pile was driven, and the work of constructing the cofferdam began.[140]

Meanwhile, the president of the Illinois and St. Louis Bridge Company sent multiple letters to the St. Louis company reiterating its exclusive rights to build the bridge. Undeterred, James moved forward with the bridge project and let the lawyers do their job. The newspapers soon began to argue that the St. Louis company did not dispute the rights of the Illinois company to build a bridge and that perhaps two bridges could be built and instead they could argue about tolls. By March 1868, the legal battle was over, and the two companies agreed to consolidate, maintaining James Eads as the chief engineer.[141]

This would only be the first of many problems to face the bridge project. The bridge James had designed would accommodate the challenges of the original bill, but engineers continually questioned the practicality and stability of the design. The proposed bridge would have three graceful steel arches, with the middle arch spanning 520 feet. Two decks would be built, one for a highway above and another two-track rail line below. The estimated cost was $5 million, with a timeline of three years to complete. James had decided to utilize a new material in his bridge, steel, which had yet to be tested in this type of structure. Engineers questioned James's ability to manufacture enough steel at the needed lengths to make the arches possible, and there were concerns about all three arches spanning more than 500 feet each, with the middle span of 520 feet being the largest ever built. Eventually, multiple engineering experts were hired to test James's calculations, and they all agreed that, in theory, the bridge should be stable.[142]

The original plan for building the massive piers involved cofferdams that would create a temporary barrier to the river and give workers a dry area to work. This process was used for the much shallower west abutment, but after seeing air caissons used in England and France, James changed his plan for the much deeper piers. Construction of the east caisson began in the spring of 1869. First, a watertight caisson was built from oak timbers and plate iron with three open-bottomed air chambers. Next, the caisson was sunk using seven-ton blocks placed on the roof. A middle shaft entrance remained so that once the caisson reached the river bottom, workers could use timber steps to reach the air chambers. An airlock was placed at the bottom of the steps where the workmen would wait until the air pressurized to match that of the air at the bottom of the caisson. Once the airlock door opened, the men proceeded into the air chamber where they worked to remove the sand by moving it through a pump system running back up through the caisson. As sand was removed, the caisson could be pushed farther down into the river until it reached bedrock.[143]

All seemed to progress as planned until workers started to become increasingly ill. It was noted in February 1870 that "occasionally some of the men are disabled by a muscular paralysis, but it soon wears off on proper treatment." A few days later, the same newspaper reported that the caisson depth had reached eighty-nine feet and that the pressure within the air chamber was about forty-one pounds, equal to nearly three normal atmospheres. It went on to report that rumors of men dying due to work in the air chambers were false and that it was impressive for a project of this size to have so few accidents. One month later, an unfortunate headline hit the papers, "Inquest at City Hospital," reporting the deaths of men who had worked in the bridge pier air chambers.[144] So much for being free from accidents.

James Riley was the first reported death on March 19, 1870. Three days later, twenty more cases were sent to the hospital, with five men eventually dying. In the news, Theodore L. Baum, John Sayers and Henry Klausman were reported to have all died from the effects of what the workmen had been calling the "bends," a nod to the stooped posture of women created by bustles and corsets. The phrase "caisson disease" wouldn't appear until 1872, when Dr. Andrew Smith began studying those effected by caisson work on the Brooklyn Bridge.[145]

James enlisted the assistance of his personal physician, Alphonse Jaminet, on March 31. By this time, eleven men had died from the effects of compressed air. Doctors at the city hospital determined that when working in the air chamber, the blood vessels would become compressed, causing their heart rate to increase. Once the workers left the chamber, the blood vessels would become distended, and all of the vital organs would be flooded with blood. Blood clots were found in the kidneys and the membranes of the brain. The spinal cords were red due to distended capillary vessels, and in some cases, the spinal cord was found to be soft and jelly-like in places.[146]

Jaminet added a floating hospital to the worksite, and the length of time workers spent in the air chamber was decreased the further the caisson descended. Jaminet insisted that all workmen rest at least one hour after being in the air chamber, and they were to be given beef tea along with their dinner while resting. He also insisted that the rate of decompression be reduced to further allow the body to adjust to the change of pressure and placed strict requirements on the physical fitness of the men who conducted the work. Men were to have a proper diet, including three meals a day; get regular sleep; and avoid alcohol. He stipulated that workers not be over the age of forty-five and excluded anyone with heart or lung disease from entering the air chamber. Workers were equipped with voltaic armor that consisted of small bands lined with thin, overlapping plates of mixed zinc and silver, worn on each wrist, around the waist and inside their stockings. While these interventions appeared to slow the rate of hospitalization, the bridge project would ultimately produce 119 severe cases and fourteen deaths from exposure to pressurized air.[147]

The next delay to hit the bridge project came in the form of an F3 tornado on the afternoon of March 8, 1871. The day began cloudy with little indication of rain, but around 1:00 p.m., the sky darkened and it began to drizzle. It wasn't until 3:00 p.m. that the storm blew in from the southwest, bringing "its fury without a moment's warning." A sheet ironworker, James Halpin, died from a blow to his head, while five additional workers were seriously injured. Across the city, another eight people died and sixty were injured. As for the bridge, the framework for carrying masonry to the east pier was demolished, and the air pump was destroyed, allowing water to refill the air chambers. They were lucky that more damage was not done, and the work was able to resume nine days later with the air chambers once again functional.[148]

The final air chamber was filled in April 1871 when the foundation to the east abutment was completed, and workers were happy to be out of the caissons and working above water level again. Attention quickly turned to the steel superstructure being built by the Keystone Bridge Company in Pittsburgh, Pennsylvania. The actual steel manufacturing work was subcontracted to the William Butcher Steel Works near Philadelphia.[149]

The early warning signs of a larger problem with the steel manufacturing process began to appear in May, as construction projects had to be put on hold for want of steel anchor bolts. Early delays were attributed to the subcontractor needing to erect specialized equipment to manufacture the twenty-two- to thirty-six-foot-long bolts. It was later reported that the first bolts tested were not strong enough and broke during testing. In addition, the testing machine broke on two separate occasions, further delaying the company's ability to test additional bolts. It was eventually determined that the carbon steel mixture used was inferior and would have to be changed.[150]

Challenges persisted when attempting to roll the thirteen-foot-long steel tubes, and after months of trial and error, the tubes produced also proved to be too weak for construction purposes. The cost of time and money started to stack up, and frustration was building. James had wanted to use chrome steel, which he had found to be superior for his needs, but had been unable to specify his preference before the steel contract had been awarded to the Keystone Bridge Company. Because the chrome steel process was patented, it was only made by one establishment. Keystone had already begun to accept bids for the manufacturing subcontract, and James felt as though he couldn't compel Keystone to use the chrome steel process over the carbon steel. All of the competitors had expressed confidence in their ability to supply a reliable quality of steel for the project, so James trusted their expertise and later regretted it. In the end, a royalty had to be paid to obtain the rights to create chrome steel, and the process of manufacturing all the steel parts resumed by December 1871.[151]

Plans for the underground railroad tunnel connecting to the bridge began in 1872, while the citizens excitedly awaited the day that the steel superstructure would start to appear across the river. Everyone hoped that the bridge would be mostly completed by the summer of 1873 and open to the public by the end of the year. Of course, nothing ever goes to plan when building something as monumental as the Eads Bridge. In June 1873, a group of steamboat men made an appeal to Washington asking for an injunction against the completion of the bridge. They argued that the arched spans of the bridge would not be high enough for larger steamboat chimneys to pass safely and would create a serious obstruction to navigating the Mississippi. James responded that it was too late for steamboat men to say that they didn't know about the planned spans when the plans had been available for viewing in the Merchant's Exchange for the past five years. Nonetheless, a board of engineering officials was appointed by the secretary of war to meet in St. Louis and assess the situation. By late August, the engineers reported that the bridge would prove a serious obstruction and must be modified. They determined that the only recourse was to create a canal through East St. Louis with a drawbridge. On November 19, the *St. Louis Republican* printed James's scathing response to the report that, in a variety of not-so-subtle ways, questioned the expertise and intelligence of the engineers involved with the review.[152]

In early 1874, the Engineers Office of the U.S. Army responded to James's rebuttal with a new plan and stated that the bridge was "admirable in some engineering features" but was not acceptable for safe navigation and that if modifications could not be made, it would have to be entirely reconstructed. It went on to explain that the simplest plan would be to remove all three arches, raise the bridge twenty-seven feet and use horizontal trusses. Through his previous work building ironclad riverboats for the navy, James had become friends with Ulysses S. Grant, who just happened to be president at the time of this trouble. James decided to visit Washington, D.C., to talk to President Grant about the situation. By April 19, 1874, the *St. Louis Republican* was reporting that the latest bridge report had been sent to the Committee on Commerce, where it would be "preserved in case it should ever be needed for historical purposes."[153]

April 19, 1874, was advertised as the day the bridge would finally be open to foot traffic. The Keystone Bridge Company was finishing its work on the project and had approved the bridge to open. Unfortunately, it changed its

Stereograph showing the construction of the Eads Bridge, 1873. *Created by Boehl and Koenig Courtesy of the Missouri Historical Society, St. Louis.*

mind the night before. The St. Louis Bridge Company, expecting a large crowd that morning, had already requested the presence of the police and was in a difficult position when people started to arrive at the bridge. Upon seeing the police, workers from the Keystone Bridge Company panicked and began to tear up planking on each side of the bridge, making it impassible to visitors. The reason for this delay and destruction could be attributed to Andrew Carnegie, who was awaiting a bonus payment for opening the bridge early. Without payment, he had decided to hold the bridge as security against the money owed to the Keystone Bridge Company. After much discussion, exchange of money and several repairs to the bridge planking, foot traffic was finally allowed to cross on May 23, 1874. It is reported that about twenty-five thousand people crossed the bridge that day.[154]

On June 4, the bridge was opened to vehicles, and about seven or eight hundred were seen crossing the bridge. Six days later, General Sherman drove the last spike into the track, and the first train containing three passenger coaches passed over the bridge several times and stopped once in the middle for a celebratory toast. One of the most publicized "tests" of the bridge occurred on June 14 when John Robinson's Circus came to town and his elephant safely crossed from Illinois to Missouri. The real final test of the bridge was made on July 2 when fourteen heavily loaded locomotives were placed on the bridge at one time—seven on the north track and seven on the south track. With government engineers present, James calculated the weight of the trains and the strength of the arches, determining that the bridge could bear the weight of three thousand pounds per foot.[155]

The grand opening for the bridge occurred with much celebration and fireworks on July 4, 1874. The bridge was the pride of the city. It had taken seven years and cost nearly $10 million to complete. While it still stands today, it has had a bad day or two in its long history. In 1878, the Illinois and St. Louis Bridge Company went bankrupt, and the bridge was auctioned on the east steps of the St. Louis courthouse for $2 million. The worst day was likely May 27, 1896, when a tornado ripped away three hundred feet of the eastern approach. Pieces of the bridge weighing several tons could be found

Pedestrians and trolley traffic on the Eads Bridge, 1903. *Courtesy of the Missouri Historical Society, St. Louis.*

Tornado destroys a section of Eads Bridge on May 27, 1896. *Photo from Richard H. Fuhrmann, courtesy of the Missouri Historical Society, St. Louis.*

one hundred feet away. Also, 255 people were killed and more than eight thousand buildings were damaged or destroyed that day. Finally, the railway tracks were removed from the bridge in 1974, and it was closed to automobile traffic in 1991. Thankfully, it found a new life when the MetroLink light-rail system opened a route from Lambert–St. Louis International Airport to East St. Louis in 1993, and automobile traffic eventually resumed.[156]

The section of town where you can still walk under the bridge displays the often disjointed atmosphere of a city as old as St. Louis. On one side is the beautifully renovated Gateway Arch National Park, and on the other side is the old riverfront district of Laclede's Landing, which has struggled to recover from years of slow decline. As the oldest section of town, ghost stories are plentiful, and it's hard to imagine such a massive structure like Eads Bridge not having a legend or two lingering around its aging limestone corners. There are stories about Native American curses, a haunted cave below the arches and even a wandering Native American boy. Some remark that the cat colony that resides at the Commercial Street archway always has fourteen cats, perhaps a reflection of the fourteen men who died building the bridge. Occasionally, you will find the remnants of spell work nearby, as some believe that there is something spiritual about this place. As for the truth of these stories, there really is no way to know, but I recommend using caution when wandering near the Eads Bridge late at night. You never know who or what you may encounter.

CHAPTER 9

CHATILLON-DEMENIL MANSION

More often than not, the stories in this book begin with a man coming from some distant place to St. Louis seeking to grow his wealth. This story is different because it begins just four miles south of St. Louis in the small town of Carondolet. Founded in 1767 by the French military officer Clement Delor de Treget, Carondelet was home to mostly farmers who supplied flour and wood to the settlers of St. Louis. The residents of Carondelet were used to hard work and knew how to live off the land. Perhaps this is why many of the well-known fur traders of that time recommended a young man from the East hire a wilderness guide from Carondelet. Henri Chatillon was born in 1813 and was the grandson of the town's founder. By the age of fifteen, Henri was working in the Rocky Mountain trails, where he was employed by fur trading companies to supply their forts with buffalo and became well respected for his ability to handle a rifle.[157] Most of what we know about Henri comes from a book written by Francis Parkman detailing his journey on the Oregon Trail in 1846, and the man he describes is what we all envision when we think of old west mountain men.

In preparing to depart St. Louis, Parkman described Henri as he appeared that morning, noting that their outfits were similar, but while Parkman was dressed to fit the role of "mountain man," Henri's clothes were purposely chosen for his line of work. Henri had prepared his horse for the expedition ahead with a plain black saddle, "holsters of heavy pistols, a blanket rolled up behind, and the trail-rope attached to his horse's neck hanging coiled in front." At the age of thirty, Henri stood six feet in height, was well muscled and confidently carried his double-barreled smooth-bore rifle, which Parkman enviously compared to his fifteen-pound Hawken rifle. Parkman noted that Henri was a simple man who could not read or write, but "he had a natural refinement and delicacy of mind."[158]

Having spent most of the last fifteen years in the western wilderness, Henri had carved out a life for himself that included a wife of the Oglala Lakota Nation by the name of Bear Robe. They had a five-year-old daughter, Emily, and Bear Robe was pregnant with their second child when Henri set out on his trip with Parkman. While on the trail, Henri received news that Bear Robe had become deathly ill and that their second daughter died shortly after birth. Bear Robe had been asking for Henri, and Parkman's group agreed to detour the few days' journey so Henri could be with her during her last moments.[159]

Bear Robe's illness had caused drastic weight loss, and she was described as skeletal-like. She had mostly lain stiffly in her makeshift bed at the Lakota camp, speaking only Henri's name before his arrival. Upon seeing Henri, she awoke with joy to see her love by her side. They spoke through the night, and the following morning, he lifted her onto a sled so she could travel to the next fort with the tribe. Unfortunately, she died soon after departing, and the tribe sent up a cry of sorrow over her body. They prepared a service for the next morning, which included a white horse to carry her to the next life. Henri, having to continue his work with Parkman, entrusted his daughter, Emily, to the care of a fellow fur trader, Joseph Bissonette.[160]

When Henri eventually returned to St. Louis, he and Parkman parted ways. Saddened by the loss of his wife, Henri commissioned a painting of himself and Bear Robe in remembrance of her spirit. The painting portrayed Bear Robe's spirit looking down on Henri and the horse that carried her to the afterlife.[161]

Two years later, Henri married his wealthy first cousin, Odile Delor Lux. Before marrying Henri, Odile had purchased twenty-one acres of land in the City Commons, and it is here that Henri built a simple two-story brick house. Over the next several years, they sold the land in segments until they finally sold the house in 1855 to Dr. Nicolas DeMenil. In 1858, Henri reclaimed his daughter, Emily, and had her baptized in Carondelet at Saint Mary and Joseph Catholic Church. Three days later, she was married to Louis Benjamin Lessert. While Henri and Odile had no children of their own, Emily gave them six grandchildren.[162]

When the DeMenil family purchased the Chatillon home, it was with the hope of escaping city life. Dr. Nicolas DeMenil was a French-born army physician who came to St. Louis in 1834. Shortly thereafter he married Emilie Chouteau. Emilie was the granddaughter of Auguste Chouteau, a successful fur trader and one of the founders of St. Louis. Her father, August Pierre Chouteau, was also a fur trader in the Native American territory of Oklahoma. Emilie's parents had a less than agreeable marriage, and her father spent most of his time at a fur trading post near present-day Saline, Oklahoma. It is believed that he had several Osage wives with multiple children and made very infrequent trips to St. Louis. After August Pierre died in 1838, the family was left with substantial amounts of debt, so Emilie mostly brought name recognition to the marriage.[163]

Dr. Nicolas DeMenil is best known for having operated a large drugstore chain after giving up his private medicine practice. Dr. DeMenil and Emilie's first home was on Seventh Street, and it is here that they celebrated the birth of their first child, also named Emilie, in September 1847. Sadly, daughter Emilie would die nine months later. Their second child, Alexander, was born in March 1849.[164]

While he had been successful in his medical business, DeMenil also had an interest in land speculation and invested in several properties around the city. When DeMenil purchased the Chatillon home, he and Emile were looking for a place to use as a summer retreat. He was later able to purchase the

The Chatillon-DeMenil Mansion. *Author's collection.*

rest of the property from Eugene Miltenberger in 1861. Emilie had always admired her cousin Henry Chouteau's Greek Revival home that once stood beside Chouteau's Pond and requested that their new home be renovated to match this style. Renovations began shortly thereafter. Architect and contractor Henry Pitcher used the original four-bedroom farmhouse as the base and added twelve feet to the western side of the house. On the east side, he added three stories, a basement and two double porches. By the time the work was completed in 1863, DeMenil had retired from medicine and was ready to move into his new home. As a Southern sympathizer, he likely felt more comfortable away from the city where Union troops were stationed. National Register records indicate that bars were likely placed on the windows as protection against soldiers or the "vagabonds of war."[165]

Dr. DeMenil lived a quiet life in which he avoided notoriety, seldom attended public gatherings and was considered to be an honest, upright and conscientious man. He loved his home and preferred spending his time either with his family or reading. His son Alexander graduated from the Academy of the Christian Brothers College in 1869. Alexander went on to earn several degrees from Washington University and Central University, Indiana, including a Bachelor and Master of Science, Master of Arts, Bachelor of Laws, Doctor of Literature and Doctor of Philosophy.[166]

In 1865, DeMenil leased a portion of his land at the corner of Seventh and Cave Streets to Charles Fritschle and Louis Zepp. This part of St. Louis had become well known for the vast network of caves below, and brewers were eager to establish their business above a cave to have easy access to the cool environment for beer storage. There was a sinkhole on this portion of the DeMenil property that allowed Fritschle and Zepp to access the cave, and from there they created two additional holes in the cave's ceiling for ice and beer casks. They named their business Minnehaha Brewery. Unfortunately, the only saloon selling their beer was owned by Louis Zepp, and when it was unable to pay its bills, DeMenil reclaimed the property.[167]

Sadly, Dr. DeMenil's wife, Emilie, passed away on March 20, 1874, at the age of sixty. Dr. DeMenil continued to reside in the home and soon filled his time with finding new ways to generate income from his real estate holdings. In 1876, DeMenil built row houses on his property along Seventh Street. The property contained ten three-story residences with seventeen flats and three stores. An advertisement in the *St. Louis Globe-Democrat* stated that the property featured "a natural sewer, or cave, opening into the river." DeMenil would later lament the placement of his new buildings, as they created an unsightly barrier between his home

Row houses at 3357–75 Seventh Street owned by Dr. N. DeMenil, 1879. *Courtesy of the Missouri Historical Society, St. Louis.*

and a river view. To rectify this problem, he moved the front entrance of the house to the Thirteenth Street side and added the formal porch with balustrades that make the building distinctive today.[168]

Meanwhile, Alexander had been practicing law since 1871 but was beginning to ponder a political career. In 1877, he ran a successful campaign and became the first Democrat elected to the House of Delegates for the Eleventh Ward. Two years later, he became the youngest member of the city council. During this time, Alexander married his first wife, Lillian May Robert, and they had one son, Henry, who was born on November 12, 1879.[169]

In July 1882, Dr. Nicolas DeMenil died at the age of sixty-nine, leaving Alexander his entire estate. Alexander and his family remained in the mansion, where he managed the family's vast amount of property and wealth. The security his father's estate afforded him, paired with the wealth he had generated in his own endeavors, allowed Alexander to eventually leave his law practice and focus on his passion for literature. Since childhood, Alexander had contributed to the Sunday newspapers, literary papers, magazines and reviews, so it had to have been a moment of pride when he became the editor for *St. Louis Magazine* in 1883. He had hopes of turning the magazine into a serious literary publication, and it soon became known for fine writing and unsparing judgement. Alexander was by all accounts a very intelligent man with refined taste who found little use in some of the more novel entertainments of the period. He had a strong distaste for ragtime culture and the authors Mark Twain and Walt Whitman.[170]

After divorcing Lillian, Alexander married Bessie Bacon in March 1886, and they celebrated the birth of Alexander's second son, George, in July 1890. He eventually stepped away from *St. Louis Magazine* in 1890 to focus on his next political endeavor. At the age of forty-four, Alexander was one of four candidates running for the St. Louis mayoral Democratic nomination. At the Democratic Convention, Alexander received the second-highest vote count of the candidates. Accepting his loss, he decided to return to his passion for literature and created his own literary journal titled *The Hesperian: A Western Quarterly Illustrated Magazine.* He was highly esteemed in the field of literature and was described as "intellectually honest, exhaustive in research, accurate in his statements, and elegant in his dictation." While he could be highly critical of other writers, he was respected by many in the literary community.[171]

In 1904, Alexander had the honor of being on the board of directors for the Louisiana Purchase Exposition World's Fair, held in St. Louis. He served as director of the French Exhibit and translator to the French dignitaries visiting the city. This was no normal fair, as the St. Louis World's Fair attracted nearly 20 million visitors over the course of seven months (April 30 to December 1, 1904). The event cost $15 million to produce and required 1,200 acres of fairgrounds to hold the 1,500 convention buildings.[172] Being involved with this enormous undertaking was likely one of the highlights of Alexander's life.

Another proud moment for Alexander had to be the day his first son, Henry, graduated from Wentworth Military Academy in 1889 and became a physician. Henry volunteered for military service in 1917 and became a captain of the U.S. Reserve Corps by 1919. It was around this same time that Alexander decided to stop publishing *The Hesperian* and settle into retirement at the age of sixty-eight.[173]

Sadly, Henry DeMenil died in December 1924, leaving behind a widow and three small children. Four years later, Alexander died at the age of seventy-nine, leaving the family home to his second son, George. George and his wife lived in the mansion until 1929. It is speculated that the family chose to move from the home due to the deterioration of the neighborhood and a general feeling that the home was no longer a good place to raise a

The Cherokee Cave Museum was open to the public from 1950 until 1961. *Courtesy of the Missouri Historical Society, St. Louis.*

family. Custodians maintained the property until 1940, when it was sold to a pharmaceutical manufacturer, Lee Hess.[174]

Hess was very interested in the Minnehaha Brewery building, which was still present on the property. He hoped to turn the cave into an underground beer garden and tourist center. First, Hess needed to remove some of the clay deposits blocking the passageways and soon discovered strange animal bones. He had them evaluated by the American Museum of Natural History, which determined them to be from an extinct flat-headed peccary, which resembled a wild boar. This prompted Hess to turn the house into a laboratory for prehistoric animals while he and his wife lived in an apartment on the second floor.[175]

Hess also decided that instead of a beer garden, the cave would become a museum. The Cherokee Cave Museum allowed visitors to enjoy the natural beauty of the cave while viewing exhibits of the Damascus Palace (previously seen at the 1904 World's Fair) and a collection of fossils found in the cave. The museum was open until 1961 and purchased soon after by the Missouri Highway Department as part of a major highway project.[176]

The route for the Ozark Expressway (Interstate 55) was to run over the entrance to the Cherokee Cave and the eastern part of the Chatillon-

DeMenil property. Since the highway department only required a portion of the property, it planned to sell the remainder (including the mansion) to a developer, who would likely demolish the building. The Landmarks Association of St. Louis quickly jumped at the chance to save the old mansion, and it became one of the first properties adopted for preservation.[177]

Since then, the house has become a museum displaying items from the DeMenil family, the 1904 World's Fair and a unique painting of a Native American woman. Over the years, a few strange stories have been told by the people who work and volunteer in this beautiful home. While there are the occasional stories of objects rearranging themselves within the house, the most striking story goes back to the 1920s, with people having reported the sight of an American Indian woman in full traditional Native dress standing on the balcony. In 1967, a strange leather-wrapped bundle was found beneath the attic floorboards. Inside was a Hawken rifle from the 1840s, and the wrapping was actually an oil painting.[178] The painting was that of a beautiful Native American woman looking downward on a forlorn man who appeared to be looking toward heaven. The painting was the one Henri Chatillon had commissioned when he returned to St. Louis in the late 1840s, and the gun belonged to Francis Parkman. Why the painting was hidden in the attic will remain a mystery, but what is known is that sightings of the Native American woman stopped shortly after the painting was hung in the home.

CHAPTER 10

LEMP MANSION

When Johann Adam Lemp arrived in St. Louis in 1838, he likely didn't expect to become the father of one of the wealthiest brewing families in America and ultimately the most legendary haunted family in the city.[179] Many German immigrants arriving in America were looking for a place to form a community and build a prosperous life for their families. Adam Lemp was looking to start over.

Adam's brewing interests started early in life, as his father was a brewer who encouraged Adam to learn the trade. Unfortunately, his father passed away when Adam was only thirteen years old. At the age of eighteen, Adam moved to Eschwege, Germany, to work in a city brewery and eventually branched out into his own business interests. He first opened a restaurant and later owned his own brewery. Unfortunately, both ventures failed, and he was feeling pressure from his many creditors. Instead of finding a way to pay off his debt, he chose to abandon his wife, Justina, and youngest son, William Jacob Lemp, along with all of his financial responsibilities.[180]

Once in St. Louis, Adam set about opening a small grocery store, A. Lemp & Company, at the corner of Sixth and Morgan. Here he sold basic supplies, manufactured vinegar and brewed beer. It was this third item that would eventually be key to Adam's success. While common in Germany, lager beer was new to Americans, and Saint Louisans came to love the effervescent, light amber beer that was made by Adam Lemp.[181]

In 1840, Adam abandoned the grocery store and established the Western Brewery at 37 South Second Street (now the location of the south leg of the Arch). Lemp's beer became so popular that large crowds could be seen regularly gathered at his brewery hall. The increased demand necessitated storing larger quantities of beer. Thankfully, in the late 1840s, Adam Lemp discovered an opening in the ground near current-day DeMenil Place and Cherokee Street. This opening led to a large cave system that spanned an extensive portion of south St. Louis. With the aid of ice cut from the frozen Mississippi River, Adam could reduce the cave's temperature from the usual fifty-five degrees to anywhere from thirty-five to forty degrees year-round. Inside a quarried portion of the cave, Adam placed several oak casks for aging his beer and his business continued to grow.[182]

Adam's twelve-year-old son, William, arrived in St. Louis in 1848 and found himself in a city well positioned for the growing beer trade. St. Louis was quickly becoming known for some of the best German lagers in the country, with forty separate facilities producing beer by 1860. After graduating from Saint Louis University, William became a foreman at the brewery and quickly learned the trade. He showed an impressive knack for brewing, but even more, he was gifted with a strong business sense. When Adam Lemp died in August 1862, William inherited half of Western Brewery, with the other half going to Charles Brauneck, Adam's grandson. Between 1864 and 1866, William bought out Brauneck and set about growing one of the largest brewing companies in America.[183]

William Lemp began planning a larger brewing facility located over the cave system that made the company's explosive growth possible. He recognized that he could eliminate some of his product transportation issues by building in this location and that there was plenty of land available for the business to grow. He also wanted to put himself in a position to meet the changing demands of business and implement new technologies as they became available.[184]

This new brewery had three above-ground levels, with the first floor containing the wash house and a large-capacity beer kettle. The second floor contained a second kettle, a hop room, a dining hall and an employee sleeping area. The third floor of the building was used for cooling the beer before being placed into fermenting tubs. Elevators moved the beer casks between floors. The brewery also contained three levels of cellar dropping into the cave system and reaching a level of fifty feet below ground. Here, beer would be stored for fermentation and aging. The complex grew over time to cover eleven city blocks, including a malt house, bottling plant, grain elevators, four icehouses and shipping yards along the Mississippi. William would become one of the first brewers to install mechanical refrigeration,

Beer wagon loaded with Lemp-Falstaff Beer parked at 1106 Chouteau Avenue, 1914. *Courtesy of the Missouri Historical Society, St. Louis.*

have his own refrigerated railroad cars and ice plants throughout the southern states, bottle his own beer and run a 350-foot-long pipeline that connected the stock house and the bottling plant. By 1877, the Western Brewery was the largest in St. Louis and ranked nineteenth nationally. By comparison, Anheuser-Busch was the thirty-second-largest brewery in the nation.[185]

William married Julia Feickert Lemp in 1861, and by all reports, the couple enjoyed a happy life together. Julia spent much of her time at home, tending to the children, and was seldom found in the society pages. William and Julia had nine children (one daughter died at birth) and resided in the home that Julia's father, Jacob Feickert, had built a short distance from the brewery in 1868. Much like the brewery business, William invested some time and money into the home and eventually expanded it into the mansion that people see today. Since he used their home as an auxiliary office for the brewery, he had a tunnel built from the basement of the house, through the caves and into the brewery. In 1892, William changed the name of the brewery from Western Brewery to William J. Lemp Brewing Company.[186]

In addition to his good business sense, William was known to be a decent, honest man who was well liked in the community. He enjoyed his work and would regularly walk through the brewery speaking with his workers. He was known to join the workers in their tasks, and employees were not afraid to approach him with suggestions or concerns. Sadly, this all began to change on December 12, 1901, when William's favorite son, Frederick, died suddenly at the age of twenty-eight from heart failure.[187] At one time, William had hoped that Frederick would be his successor in the brewing business.

Devastated by this loss, his employees noticed a change in William. While he still walked through the plant regularly, it was more to pass the time, and he seemed to have lost his passion for the day-to-day activities of the brewery. The second blow came on January 1, 1904, when William's closest friend, Captain Frederick Pabst, died. William was deeply affected by this loss and was noted to primarily sit in his office most days fidgeting with objects as if nervous and trying to distract himself.[188]

On the morning of February 13, 1904, William woke at 7:00 a.m. and ate breakfast. He then informed a servant that he wasn't feeling well, but nothing else seemed out of the ordinary. At roughly 9:30 a.m., William shot himself in the head using his .38-caliber Smith & Wesson revolver. A servant heard the muffled sound and ran upstairs to find the door locked. She soon returned with William's sons, Billy and Edwin, who broke down the door and found their father lying on the bed in a pool of blood, still breathing but unconscious. William J. Lemp died at 10:15 a.m., becoming the first of the Lemp family to die by suicide.[189]

In the wake of William's death, his eldest son, William (Billy) Lemp Jr., became president of the brewing company. Billy was thirty-seven years old and well known in the city as a playboy who was happy to spend his money entertaining himself and his friends. He was also described as cold, serious and unforgiving. In 1899, Billy married Lillian Handlan, reportedly a very popular, beautiful and daring socialite in St. Louis at the time.[190] The two made an interesting pair, and the details of their life together were often the topic of gossip and notes in the societal pages of the newspaper.

The city's obsession with the couple became increasingly apparent when the papers began to report that Billy had moved out of the couple's home in October 1906, and Lillian later filed for divorce. Lillian, also known as the Lavender Lady for her choice of clothing color, wanted custody of their only child, William J. Lemp III. She argued that Billy had prevented her from raising her son with any religion and had "taught him profanity and cruelty." Further, she accused him of abuse and entertaining other women in their home when she was away.[191] The trial was front-page news, and residents turned out in droves to hear the sordid details of the couple's relationship.

Lillian claimed that Billy would sleep with a gun under his pillow pointed at her head. Meanwhile, Billy complained that Lillian conducted herself inappropriately by wearing lavender clothing (which he did not like) to get attention and smoking. He also presented a letter that he had found written by Lillian addressed to "My Dear Little Pal" that he claimed proved she was involved with another man. Lillian argued that she had written the letter to make Billy jealous and left it where he could find it.[192]

The largest contention was the religious upbringing of their son. Lillian was Catholic and wanted the same for her child. Billy didn't want his son raised within any religion. He went as far as to have her unknowingly sign a document that forbade her from raising any of their children in the Catholic Church. This was in direct conflict with a document he had signed before their marriage giving her the ability to raise their children as Catholics. On February 18, 1909, the front page of the *St. Louis Post-Dispatch* announced "Lemp Rejoices at Divorce for Lavender Lady." Lillian was awarded $6,000 per year in alimony and control of the education and religious upbringing of their son. As Billy was a very wealthy man, Lillian was not happy with the alimony award. So she motioned for a retrial, and her case was eventually heard by the Missouri Supreme Court, from which she was awarded a gross alimony of $100,000, the largest to have ever been awarded in Missouri.[193]

After the trial, Billy decided to get out of the public eye and spend more time outside of the city. In 1910, he built his beautiful country home, Alswel, on the bluffs of the Meramec River. Billy's brother, Edwin, also built a home nearby named Cragwold. By 1914, Alswel had become Billy's full-time residence, and the Lemp Mansion was remodeled into the new offices for the William J. Lemp Brewing Company. In 1915, Billy married Ellie Limberg, the wealthy widow of brewer Rudolph Limberg. Her father, Casper Koehler, was president of the Columbia Brewery of St. Louis.[194]

While Billy was getting his personal life back in order, he let the upkeep of the brewery slide. The equipment was becoming outdated, and the plant was showing signs of age. He stuck rigidly to the brewing methods of his father and refused to integrate new ideas into the plant, allowing other breweries to surpass Lemp Beer as the most popular beverage in the city. All the while, the American Anti-Saloon League had been working silently in the background of political affairs. It started to have success with individual states enacting prohibitions, but Missouri stood firm defeating proposals in 1916 and again in 1918. Unfortunately for Billy and his brewery, the league was also making headway inside Congress and was able to get the Senate to pass a resolution containing a proposed Prohibition amendment. A modified version was passed by the House of Representatives on December 17, 1917, and it was then issued to the states for ratification. On January 16, 1919, the Eighteenth Amendment was ratified and was set to become effective on January 16, 1920. Congress passed the National Prohibition Act on October 28, 1919, which provided guidelines for the federal enforcement of Prohibition.[195]

With the Eighteenth Amendment ratified, many breweries quickly transitioned their plants to produce other products, one of which was called near beer in which they attempted to replicate beer without the alcohol. Lemp Brewery joined this movement and produced a beverage called "Cerva." Citing high overhead, brewing costs and low sales as issues, Lemp Brewery stopped producing the near beer in June 1919. With the start of Prohibition looming and nothing to produce, the brewery promptly closed. Reports indicate that employees showed up for work one morning to find the gates locked.[196] They had not been informed of the closure and were left to find work elsewhere.

Away from the brewery, Billy's youngest sister, Elsa, was having problems of her own. She had been awarded a divorce from her husband, Thomas Wright, in February 1919 due to claims of indifference and being absent from their home. Her doctor argued that Elsa had been suffering from postpartum depression and having emotional issues that were intensified by her husband's absence. Strangely, she and Mr. Wright reconciled shortly after their divorce and remarried on March 8, 1920. Twelve days later in their Central West End home, Mr. Wright found Elsa in her bed with a gunshot wound near her heart and a revolver lying beside her. There was no suicide note, and none of the staff present could remember any instance in which Elsa said she wished to end her life. While Elsa's brothers, Edwin and Billy, were quick to arrive on the scene, no one called the police to report the death.[197] Elsa was the second member of the Lemp family to die by suicide.

Billy found himself falling into a deep depression as time passed. The brewery was vacant, with weeds growing around it, and he had just lost his sister. He was soon approached by his good friend, Joseph Griesedieck, with an offer to purchase the Falstaff (Lemp) logo. Griesedieck believed that Prohibition would be short-lived, and he planned to use the Falstaff logo and

Corner of Twelfth and Olive, 1919. Sign reads, "Bone dry forever / Buy now for the rest of your life." *Courtesy of the Missouri Historical Society, St. Louis.*

name to build a new brewery. Billy did not share Griesedieck's optimism for the future of brewing and was opposed to the idea of anyone other than a Lemp family member using the Falstaff brand. After some consideration and assurances from Griesedieck, Billy eventually agreed to sell Falstaff to his friend for $25,000. He also decided that it was time to get rid of the brewery itself, so he put it up for auction. On June 28, 1922, the once highly

Lemp Brewery Bottling Department, date unknown. *Photo by Emil Boehl Courtesy of the Missouri Historical Society, St. Louis.*

acclaimed brewery was sold. Having once been valued at $7 million, Billy Lemp was saddened to see the brewery sold at auction in five parts, with the largest portion going to the International Shoe Company for $588,500. Billy had hoped to receive a minimum of $1,050,000 for the complex and was enraged that his legacy had sold for eight cents on the dollar.[198]

Having seen the end of the legendary brewery, Billy fell further into despair. The office remained open and Billy and his staff continued to attend to business, but things had drastically changed. Billy was noticed to be erratic, complaining of poor health and nervousness. He had a few short hospital stays due to ill health and had talked about liquidating the business by selling off the saloons and any associated land so he could travel and relax. He even put his country home, Alswel, up for sale for $175,000 (about $3.2 million in 2024).[199]

On December 29, 1922, members of the brewery office staff arrived to find Billy sitting at his desk with his forehead in his hands. The staff reported chatting briefly with him before going about their work. Shortly thereafter, Billy was found lying on his back on the floor with a .38-caliber revolver lying beside him.[200] He had shot himself in the heart and became the third member of the family to die by suicide.

When Prohibition was repealed in 1933, Griesedieck made good on his word, opened the Falstaff Brewing Corporation and obtained federal permit no. 1 to legally brew beer. Meanwhile, William J. Lemp III was finding himself in less than ideal circumstances. Alswel had been auctioned after Billy's death, and the mortgage was held by the Methodist Episcopal Church. Willam III and his wife, Agnes, had been living in the home since the 1930s but soon found themselves unable to pay the church. They ultimately lost the Alswel estate. In 1937, his marriage ended, and his ex-wife ended up in such financial distress that she sold several pieces of her jewelry and worked at a department store downtown.[201]

In 1939, William III attempted to restore the family brewing legacy by agreeing to license the name of Lemp to Central Breweries Inc. of East St. Louis, Illinois. The brewery would pay royalties to William III on all beer brewed using the "Lemp" name. In October of that year, Central changed its name to William J. Lemp Brewing Company and launched a marketing campaign heralding the return of Lemp beer. At first, sales were good, but by September 1940, things had changed. The company had racked up a massive amount of debt, and by 1941, it was bankrupt. Sadly, things did not improve for William III, and on March 12, 1943, he died suddenly at the age of forty-two of a cerebral hemorrhage while walking down the sidewalk.[202]

Another of William J. Lemp Sr.'s sons, Charles Lemp, took up residence in the family mansion in 1929. Considered by some as a rather peculiar figure, Charles was a bachelor who lived alone. While he had enjoyed a life filled with successful businesses, travel and politics, his later years found him arthritic and very ill. He became reclusive and terrified of germs to the point that he refused to shake hands with anyone, showered multiple times a day and insisted that anything from outside the mansion be washed before he handled it. His only companions were his two servants (the Bittners), a parrot and a German shepherd named Cerva.[203]

Charles eventually got to a point that he could not utilize the stairs and moved from his second-floor suite to the first floor. His room was in the back of the house, with the adjoining atrium serving as his office. On the morning of May 10, 1949, the fourth and final Lemp family suicide occurred. At roughly 6:30 a.m., Albert Bittner prepared breakfast for Charles and placed it on the office desk adjoining Charles's bedroom. At the time, the bedroom door was closed, and Albert left without checking on Charles. When he returned around 8:00 a.m. to pick up the dishes, he found the breakfast untouched. He then opened the bedroom door and found Charles lying in bed with a bullet wound in the head and a .38-caliber Army Colt revolver in his right hand. A suicide note dated May 9, 1949, was found simply saying, "In case I am found dead blame it on no one but me."[204]

Charles Lemp had already made his funeral arrangements. He had stipulated that upon his death his body should be taken immediately to Missouri Crematory. He asked that he not be bathed, changed or clothed and that no services were to be held nor any death notice published. He requested that his ashes be placed in a wicker box and buried on the farm. Edwin Lemp picked up his brother's remains on May 11, 1949, and the final resting place of Charles remains unknown.[205]

The Lemp Mansion next became a boardinghouse with rooms for eighteen tenants. The building slowly began to decay and fell into disrepair. In the 1960s, the construction of Interstate 55 threatened the mansion, and ultimately the house was saved in conjunction with the Chatillon-DeMenil Mansion; unfortunately, much of the grounds were demolished. The mansion was purchased in 1975 by Richard Pointer with plans to open a restaurant.[206] Today, people regularly visit Lemp Mansion to have a nice meal, party on Halloween, spend the night in one of the restored rooms or look for the spirits of the long-lost Lemp family.

The owners and visitors alike report many strange incidents within the mansion walls, such as doors opening and closing, the sound of the

Lemp Mansion. *Author's collection.*

piano being played, objects moving on their own, disembodied voices and the sound of horse hooves by the carriage house. And then there are the apparitions. A dark-haired man has been seen sitting in the dining room, a well-dressed man in a dark suit stands near the basement fireplace, the smoky and transparent image of a woman in a white dress descends the front stairs, a man walks down the hall and into the William Lemp Suite and a small boy looks out the windows of the top floor of the home.[207]

On one team visit to the mansion, we were wrapping up for the night, and a team member walked into the basement to clear the area. The next thing we all know, she screamed, and there was a thunder of footsteps from all points in the house running to the basement. When we arrived, she appeared shaken and about to hyperventilate. She said that something dark came flying past her face. The team immediately set about looking for anything that could have caused it. She had been alone in the basement, and she swore that it looked like a face. What did she see that night? We still don't know. Was it a member of the Lemp family, someone else who resided in the home or even something that came along with one of the many visitors to the mansion every year? It's hard to say, but it is very likely that the Lemp Mansion has a variety of spirits within its walls.

CHAPTER 11

SAINT LOUIS UNIVERSITY
AND THE EXORCISM

As displayed by many of the stories of St. Louis, the city grew in a fairly haphazard way, with the small government doing its best to spend as little money as possible. One way that early cities like St. Louis advanced was through the efforts of religious organizations. For missionaries to spread their religion to new areas, they often needed to teach people how to read and care for their ill. This led to the formation of schools and hospitals. When representatives of the Catholic Church arrived in St. Louis, they recognized an opportunity and quickly set about establishing several institutions that remain to this day.

Before Bishop William DuBourg's arrival in 1818, residents of St. Louis were celebrating Mass in a small log church constructed in 1776. At the first meeting with parishioners, DuBourg laid out his plans to build a church, open schools and send missionaries to nearby Native American tribes. Eager to get started, Catholic and non-Catholic residents pledged funds to build the first brick church in the city.[208]

At the corner of Second and Market Streets, construction of the first Basilica of St. Louis, King of France (now known as the Old Cathedral), began on March 29, 1818. As he told the parishioners in the first meeting, DuBourg wasn't just interested in building churches—he wanted to make sure that the diocese was providing proper education to the people of the region. He opened a school for boys in the home of Madame Alvarez on Church Street in November of 1818 and named it Saint Louis Academy. Tuition was twelve dollars each term, and classes included Latin, English,

Drawing of St. Louis College. *Courtesy of the Saint Louis University Archives.*

French, arithmetic, mathematics and geography. In 1820, it was renamed Saint Louis College and relocated to Washington Avenue, becoming known as the first institution of higher learning west of the Mississippi River.[209]

In 1823, DuBourg invited the Maryland Jesuits to staff missions to the Native Americans and establish a house in Florissant for this work. He also asked the Jesuits if they would take over leadership of the college, but the Jesuits originally declined the offer. In 1826, DuBourg decided to close the college, as the priests struggled to balance their duties between the school and the church. Thankfully, Father Saulnier and Bishop Rosati refused to let the school die and kept things afloat long enough for the Jesuits to take over in 1829. The school received a formal charter from the State of Missouri and was renamed Saint Louis University in 1832, becoming the first university west of the Mississippi River. The university went on to boast several firsts, including the first graduate programs (1832), medical school (1836) and law department (1843) west of the Mississippi.[210]

Saint Louis University eventually moved to its current location at the corner of Grand and Lindell in 1888. This is where the university marked many more milestones, including a strange event marked on the official university timeline for the year 1949: "Jesuits from Saint Louis University perform the religious rite that becomes the basis of 'The Exorcist' book and movie."[211] It is unlikely that this was something Bishop DuBourg had foreseen when he invited the Jesuits to the city, but he likely wouldn't have been surprised that this group would choose to help someone in dire need no matter how strange the request.

On March 5, 1949, Ronald Hunkeler and his family traveled from their home in Mount Rainer, Maryland, to St. Louis in search of relief from the strange occurrences that had been plaguing Ronald since mid-January. The trouble began with the sound of dripping inside the walls, then pictures shaking, scratching, squeaking shoes marching beside Ronald's bed, knocking inside the walls and then the shaking of his mattress. The problem wasn't confined to his home, as Ronald experienced problems in class—his desk would begin shaking and moving around the classroom with him in it. He eventually needed to take a leave of absence from school and spent much of his time at home. Things quickly escalated to objects flying across rooms, tables and chairs tipping over and eventually scratches that appeared to spell words across Ronald's flesh.[212]

Early on, the family called in an exterminator to check for rodents in the walls, with nothing to be found. As things progressed, they tried getting help from a variety of professionals, including physicians, psychologists, psychiatrists and a Lutheran minister. The minister explained that the Lutheran Church did not have a system for dealing with situations such as Ronald's and that the family would likely need to consult a Catholic priest.[213] The idea of an exorcism had been floated by the minister, but this was not a rite he could conduct.

By late February, the scratches were getting worse, and Ronald's parents started making plans to visit family in St. Louis. They hoped that they could outrun whatever was torturing their son. Ronald's mom believed that the problem stemmed from the death of his aunt who had lived in St. Louis. The aunt was deeply invested in Spiritualism and had taught Ronald how to use a Ouija board to communicate with the dead. After her passing, Ronald spent some time using the board on his own.[214] The problem with this theory was that the aunt died *after* the activity had already begun. This didn't stop Ronald's mom from believing that the connection was with the now-deceased aunt.

On Monday, March 7, Ronald's family arrived in St. Louis and were invited to stay with family in Normandy (a town north of St. Louis). The family was Lutheran and had reportedly asked for advice from their minister before Ronald's arrival. The minister told them that he was unable to assist in this situation and advised them to consult a Catholic priest. Hoping for the best, they accepted Ronald's family into their home. Everything appeared to be fine at first, but as the first night wore on, Ronald began to experience painful scratches on his body, shaking of his bed and scratching on his mattress. Unsure how to handle the situation, Ronald's family relocated to the home of their Catholic relatives in the St. Louis suburb of Bel-Nor. Once again, Ronald experienced scratching, his mattress shaking and a stool being moved several feet away from the bed.[215]

One witness to the events on this night was Ronald's cousin, a student at Saint Louis University. She was concerned by the things that had happened in her family's home and requested a meeting with her favorite Jesuit professor, Father Raymond J. Bishop, SJ. Father Bishop listened to her concerns for Ronald and her family. She let him know that the Lutheran minister had indicated a need for a Catholic priest to potentially perform an exorcism. Father Bishop felt moved to help the family and reassured the cousin that he would do what he could, promising to be in touch as soon as possible. He consulted another Jesuit about the cousin's story and was encouraged to continue to monitor the situation, collect as much information as possible and seek counsel from the president of the university, Father Paul Reinert, SJ. Taking this advice, Father Bishop scheduled a meeting with Father Reinert and then called the cousin to plan a visit to the home so he could speak with Ronald directly and perform a house blessing.[216]

On Wednesday, March 9, Father Bishop arrived at the Bel-Nor home and was introduced to the family. He questioned Ronald's parents on the events that had led to their arrival in St. Louis and then sat down to speak with Ronald. Father Bishop noted that Ronald appeared to be an average thirteen-year-old boy. As the evening wore on, he had a hard time reconciling the quiet boy sitting before him with the stories he had heard from the family. Despite his misgivings, Father Bishop went ahead and performed a blessing of the entire house and a special blessing in the room in which Ronald would be sleeping. He pinned a relic of St. Margaret Mary to the boy's pillow, and then Ronald prepared for bed. Once settled, Father Bishop observed the mattress begin to move back and forth. He sprinkled holy water on the bed in the form of the cross, and the movement ceased briefly but began again. Ronald cried out in pain, and a brief investigation by his mom revealed zig-zag scratches on Ronald's abdomen. This went on for some time, but eventually, the mattress shaking stopped. Father Bishop was taken back to the university, where he could reflect on everything he had witnessed that night.[217]

Father Bishop discussed the situation with the university president, Father Reinert, who was hesitant to get involved. The university was already in a precarious situation as it pushed for desegregation of the city of St. Louis. In 1944, Saint Louis University became the first university in Missouri to desegregate, and three years later, with some pressure from the university's Institute of Social Order, the archbishop of St. Louis, Reverend Joseph Ritter, agreed to desegregate the archdiocese. The archbishop and Father Reinert had a tenuous relationship, and having to request permission for an exorcism to occur at the university felt like a step too far for the uneasy truce. Ultimately, Father Reinert was able to remove himself from the decision since his position with the university was purely administrative, and Father Bishop was advised that he would have to request permission from the archbishop on his own if he thought an exorcism was needed.[218]

Father William S. Bowdern, SJ, former pastor of St. Francis Xavier College Church. *Courtesy of the Saint Louis University Archives.*

With everything that he had seen, Father Bishop felt that he needed help deciding what to do next and took his concerns to his friend, fifty-two-year-old Father William S. Bowdern, SJ. Father Bowdern was not a faculty member of Saint Louis University but instead was the pastor at the college church, St. Francis Xavier. In addition to serving the university faculty and students, the church served the Catholic community near the university. Father Bowdern had served as a U.S. Army chaplain in Europe, China, Burma and India, which gave him a reputation for steady nerves and fearlessness in the face of uncertainty. After hearing the events witnessed on Wednesday night, Father Bowdern agreed to accompany Father Bishop to speak with the family on the night of Friday, March 11.[219]

During the daytime hours, the house was quiet and peaceful. Ronald would read his comic books or play board games with family members. Unfortunately, things changed drastically once Ronald lay down in bed. On Friday night, he retired to his room at 11:00 p.m. and promptly called down to everyone that something had been thrown across the room. Upon reaching Ronald, it was discovered that the St. Margaret Mary relic Father Bishop had left on Wednesday had been thrown against the mirror. Ronald also had a cross mark painfully scored on his left forearm. Father Bowdern proceeded to pray while blessing Ronald with a relic from the forearm of

St. Francis Xavier. After the blessing, the group went back downstairs to discuss the history of the case. Father Bowdern insisted on collecting as much information as possible before making any decision about what should happen next. While the adults were talking, a loud crash was heard from upstairs, where a bottle of holy water had been thrown from a table. Father Bowdern placed his rosary around Ronald's neck and recited the rosary followed by another blessing. Feeling that the activity had subsided for the night, the priests left around 12:30 a.m. Unfortunately, shortly after they left, a heavy scraping noise was heard as a bookcase moved from alongside the bed to in front of the doorway. The bed began shaking, and the scratching resumed.[220] The family's terror was nowhere near ending.

Fathers Bishop and Bowdern returned to the university and spent most of that weekend researching demonic possession, exorcisms and the requirements for conducting one. They ultimately concluded that they needed to reach out to the archbishop, Reverend Joseph Ritter, to request that a priest be selected to conduct an exorcism. A letter of request arrived at the archbishop's office on Monday, March 14, and he promptly approved the request with two stipulations. One, that the exorcism be conducted by Father Bowdern, and two, that the priests never speak of the exorcism to anyone. Despite this request, Father Bowdern did ask Father Bishop to keep a written record of the process as they had struggled to find any firsthand accounts of anyone who had performed an exorcism. Father Bowdern believed that having the "Exorcist Diary" preserved in the Jesuit records would be helpful to anyone placed in a similar situation in the future. With all of this decided, the priests requested that twenty-six-year-old Walter Halloran drive them to the Bel-Nor home on Wednesday, March 16, to begin the ritual.[221]

Halloran was a young Jesuit studying at the university. He often assisted Father Bowdern with errands around town and was not surprised to be asked to drive the priests to their appointment. He was surprised when he was asked to come into the house because Father Bowdern was going to perform an exorcism and that someone was needed to hold the boy down if he became overly agitated. Halloran did not question the request and followed Father Bowdern into the home. Shortly after 10:30 p.m. that night, Father Bowdern led Ronald through a process to examine his conscience and make an act of contrition. Once this was completed, Father Bishop, Halloran, Ronald's mother, his aunt and his uncle entered the room, knelt beside the bed and began praying. After this was completed, Father Bowdern began to read from the *Rituale Romanum* and recited prayers of exorcism.

Almost immediately, scratches began to appear on Ronald's stomach, legs, thighs, back, chest, face and throat. Some of these scratches appeared to form words such as *hell* and *go*. Four markings were interpreted as "X," which they would later believe to be an answer to the question of when the entity might leave (ten days).[222]

Eventually, Ronald appeared to fall asleep as the priests continued to pray. This peace was short-lived. As prayers to St. Michael began, Ronald sat up, laughed and began pounding his fists into the back of his bed and then a pillow. He swung his arms in violence and claimed to be fighting a large red devil. Ronald had to be held down as he threatened violence and spat at everyone in the room. He would occasionally slumber, then wake up thirsty and then become violent again. This cycle continued from midnight until around five o'clock in the morning, when he awoke, appearing weak and unable to sit up on his own. He began to sing in a high-pitched voice and swung his arms as if interpreting the song. The prayers continued, and by seven-thirty that morning, Ronald had finally fallen into a natural sleep.[223]

For the next four nights, Father Bowdern and Father Bishop would go to the Bel-Nor home with the aid of Walter Halloran to continue the rite of exorcism. The scratching, yelling, singing and spitting would become regular occurrences, with the addition of vulgar language. By Monday, March 21, Ronald's family was so exhausted that his mother had to be taken to see a doctor. It was decided that in order to give the family peace, Ronald needed to be moved to a hospital. Understanding the need to keep the exorcism quiet, Father Bowdern requested assistance from the Alexian brothers. While not Jesuits, the brothers were well trusted to care for any man in need, and that included priests who tended to indulge in too much alcohol. The Alexian Brothers Hospital was located in South St. Louis, and Father Bowdern requested a bed in one of the security rooms for Ronald. There were leather straps on the bed, bars on the windows and no doorknob on the inside of the large, heavy door. Ronald's father accompanied the group that night, and the exorcism continued. This night saw very little agitation from Ronald, and this may have been due to his inability to relax in what was likely a very frightening space. By 11:30 p.m., the prayers had concluded, and the priests left Ronald and his father to pray. Ronald fell into a normal sleep shortly thereafter. He returned to Bel-Nor the next morning.[224]

Unfortunately, the next night was not as peaceful, and the usual prayers commenced around 11:00 p.m., punctuated with bouts of bed shaking.

Alexian Brother's Hospital, 1872. *Courtesy of the Missouri Historical Society, St. Louis.*

While not as intense as before, the activity continued to cause distress in the home, so Father Bowdern arranged for Ronald to stay with him at the church rectory. Once again, Ronald's father came along, and two beds were provided so father and son could be near each other throughout their stay. From March 23 through March 25, the exorcism continued at the rectory. As before, Ronald's days would be peaceful, and at night he would become violent. The evenings now included not just scratching, yelling, singing, spitting and vulgar language but also insults, urination and pretending to masturbate. There are stories from this time of Jesuits living in neighboring Verhaegen Hall who would hear tortured screams, wild laughter and foul smells coming from the rectory.[225] If true, Father Bowden was struggling to keep the exorcism a secret.

Believing that whatever was possessing Ronald would leave ten days after the start of the exorcism, Father Bowden was hopeful that Friday, March 25, would mark the end of the difficult ordeal. That night, Ronald tossed and turned as the priests prayed. After midnight, he began moving more fitfully, cursed his father and spat at him. He then proceeded to kick a priest and then kick a chair across the room before falling into a deep sleep. On

Saint Louis University College Church Rectory just before razing, 1966. *Photo by Father Boleslaus Lukaszewski, courtesy of the Saint Louis University Archives.*

Saturday, he returned to the house in Bel-Nor. Father Bowdern blessed the house, and no activity was reported for five nights.[226] The family started to believe that things would go back to normal.

On the night of Thursday, March 31, Ronald came down from bed complaining that he felt sick and that his feet were alternating between hot and cold. His mom assisted him back to bed, and as he settled in, the bed began to shake. He moved his finger across the sheet as if using it to write and told his family that he was reading from a blackboard. He told them the writing said, "I will stay 10 days, but will return in 4." The family quickly called Father Bowdern, and he arrived at the home with Father O'Flaherty around one o'clock in the morning. As he began the rite of exorcism, Ronald requested a pencil and was granted this request. He wrote on the headboard and the sheets. Eventually, someone went to get large sheets of wrapping paper and fastened them to the bed. Ronald wrote many things throughout the night but mostly repeated the ten-day statement, drew multiple "X"s and wrote, "I will answer to the name of Spite."[227]

Ronald had begun learning the Catholic faith during his waking hours, and his family agreed to have him baptized into the church. On April 1, the family loaded Ronald into the car and drove into the city. Ronald suddenly went into one of his fits, grabbing the steering wheel of the car, and his uncle was forced to pull off the road. The family struggled to get Ronald into the back of the car, where they could restrain him for the remainder of the trip, but he got loose at least once and was able to grab his aunt while she was driving. When the family finally arrived, it was decided that the baptism could not be administered inside the church, and Ronald was carried to the third-floor rectory room in which he had previously stayed. Father Bowdern chose to use the procedure for baptism of infants to reduce the need for Ronald to respond, but he did ask, "Dost thou renounce Satan?" four times before Ronald was able to reply, "I do renounce him." After the baptism was completed, the exorcism prayers began again, with the usual spitting, cursing and violent responses from Ronald.[228]

The next morning did not follow the usual peaceful routine, and Ronald threw things about the room. He settled long enough to go through a confession, but when it was time to take his first communion, Ronald spit it out at least five times. After two hours of trying, they finally were able to get him to take communion. He then got dressed and prepared to return to Bel-Nor. Father O'Flaherty had agreed to drive the boy home and was thanked for this by being attacked by Ronald as he drove. Ronald had to be pulled off, and the remainder of the ride was less than pleasant for everyone involved. When Ronald was aware again, he begged his family to take him back to Maryland.[229] He wanted to go home. The situation clearly had not been resolved, but the family agreed that they needed to give their relatives back some peace and try to return to their life.

On Monday, April 4, Ronald, his parents and Father Bowdern boarded a train to Washington, D.C. Father Bowdern hoped to find someone in the area who could continue the exorcism closer to the family's home. He first met with the chancellor of the Archdiocese of Washington and received approval to continue the exorcism, but no priest was willing or able to assume responsibility of the case. Father Bowdern was unable to stay in Washington long term, so he needed to find someone to care for Ronald. Due to the frequent violent outbursts, the family decided that Ronald shouldn't stay at home, and the search for a suitable hospital began. Father Bowdern contacted several hospitals in the area, but no one was willing to accept the burden. The nuns with the Daughters of Charity were initially willing to take Ronald, but the doctors refused to allow a patient to be admitted for treatment of exorcism. Finally, Father Bowdern called the Alexian brothers in St. Louis and received permission to bring Ronald back to the hospital. Less than a week after leaving St. Louis, Father Bowdern and Ronald returned to the Alexian Brothers Hospital on Sunday, April 10.[230]

Over the next eight days, Ronald would live among the Alexian brothers. During the day, he would help them with their chores, and at night, Father Bowdern would arrive to continue the rite of exorcism. Like the nights that had come before, Ronald would yell profanities, spit at the priests, be scratched and pretend to perform sexual acts. The Monday after Easter was to be the worst and, thankfully, the last day of the ordeal. Ronald began having fits at eight o'clock that morning that included kicking one of the brothers and throwing a bottle of holy water across the room. The violence only increased throughout the day, and when Father Bowdern arrived, he probably was not thinking that this would be the day that his long hours of prayer would finally pay off. Father Bowdern was exhausted. His brother, a physician, had noted not just the weight Father Bowdern had lost but also the swelling around his eyes and boils on his arms. Thankfully, at 10:45 p.m., everything changed.[231]

Father Bowdern had uttered the last "Amen" in the ritual, and the room had become quiet. Ronald was still in his bed and suddenly took a deep breath. The words that came from his mouth did not sound like his own, and in a very loud, clear, masculine voice, he claimed to be St. Michael the Archangel and stated, "I command you Satan, and the other evil spirits to leave the body in the name of Dominus. Immediately! Now, now, now!" Ronald's body then went into violent convulsions. Once the fight was over, he fell quiet for a few moments before sitting up, smiling and proclaiming, "He's gone!" He spent a few more days with the Alexian brothers, but soon it was determined that he was well enough to go home.[232] The episodes did not return.

Once home, Ronald was able to go back to school and graduate like every other normal kid in his class. He went on to college and became a NASA engineer, where he patented technology to make space shuttle panels resistant to extreme heat. After nearly forty years of work, he retired from NASA in 2001. None of his colleagues knew about his past, and Ronald did his best to avoid having anyone discover that he had been the boy who inspired the horrific exorcism story. Ronald died shortly before his eighty-sixth birthday in May 2020.[233]

As for the aftereffects of the exorcism on St. Louis, students at Saint Louis University are occasionally found wandering the upper floors of DuBourg Hall chasing rumors of demons. Seniors tell tales to the freshman, often proclaiming that there is a room on the fourth floor where a light is kept on, and the only time the door is unlocked is to change the lightbulb. Other students say that this all happened in Verhaegen Hall or the College Church basement or perhaps Jesuit Hall. The truth is that the church rectory was torn down in 1966 to make way for a new building.[234] The house in Bel-Nor has been the scene of many paranormal television shows and has had its own exorcism. Most people who have been in the house claim that there is nothing strange about it at all and that the claims of haunting are unfounded.

And what of the Alexian Brothers Hospital? I've heard rumors that Ronald's room was locked and never used again. All of the furniture was left in place, and no one ventured into the room until the day the building was slated to be demolished in 1978. At that time, a maintenance worker removed the furniture and found a copy of the "Exorcist Diary" in a bedside drawer. The diary ended up in the hands of Father Walter Halloran, and the whereabouts of the furniture is unknown.[235] Many claim that strange things still happen in the location of the old building and that a portal can be found in the parking lot of the current hospital. What we know for certain is that the exorcism left a curious mark on the university and the city of St. Louis.

NOTES

Chapter 1

1. Winch, *Clamorgans*, 7–8.
2. Ibid., 13.
3. Ibid., 14; Winch, *Colored Aristocracy of St. Louis*, 23; Winch, *Clamorgans*, 42–43.
4. Winch, *Clamorgans*, 43.
5. Ibid., 43–46.
6. Ibid., 46–47.
7. Winch, *Colored Aristocracy*, 22–25; Winch, *Clamorgans*, 81–82.
8. Winch, *Colored Aristocracy*, 50–51; Winch, *Clamorgans*, 49.
9. Winch, *Clamorgans*, 49.
10. Ibid., 44–55.
11. Ibid., 56–58.
12. Ibid., 59–62.
13. Ibid., 62–66; *George Speers, et al. v. Peter Chouteau*, 684, St. Louis Chancery Court File, November Term, (1841).
14. Hebrank, *Geologic Story of the St. Louis Riverfront*, 13; Gordon, *Fire, Pestilence, and Death*, 117.

Chapter 2

15. Foley, "John B.C. Lucas."
16. Ibid., "Auguste Chouteau."

17. Ibid.
18. Moore, *Old Courthouse*, 2–3.
19. Ibid., 3.
20. Ibid, 3.
21. Ibid, 3–4.
22. Simmons, "Henry Singleton's Architectural Legacy," 7.
23. Ibid., 7–8.
24. Ibid., 8–9.
25. Moore, *Old Courthouse*, 5–6.
26. Ibid., 7.
27. Ibid., 6, 31, 33.
28. Ibid., 33–35.
29. Ibid., 10–11; "Administrator's Sale of Slaves," *St. Louis Globe-Democrat*, April 27, 1853.
30. Moore, *Old Courthouse*, 13, 16.
31. Robert S. Mitchell, letter to the editor, *St. Louis Globe-Democrat*, January 16, 1857; Robert S. Mitchell, "To the Tax-Payers of St. Louis County," *Daily Missouri Republican*, January 16, 1859; Moore, *Old Courthouse*, 16; Justice, letter to the editor, *Daily Missouri Republican*, June 27, 1858; "Ballot Stuffing Cloaked by the County Court—Two of the Judges Accessory to the Election Frauds," *St. Louis Globe-Democrat*, August 21, 1858; Simmons, "Henry Singleton's Architectural Legacy," 10.
32. Moore, *Old Courthouse*, 18; Mitchell, "To the Tax-Payers".
33. Moore, *Old Courthouse*, 18.
34. Ibid., 19–23.
35. Ibid., 21, 27.
36. Institute of Museum and Library Services Missouri State Library, "Missouri Drake Constitution Ratified"; Moore, *Old Courthouse*, 14.
37. Moore, *Old Courthouse*, 27–28; Gesley, "Old Courthouse in St. Louis."

Chapter 3

38. Peterson, "Manuel Lisa's Warehouse," 59; Truteau, *Fur Trader on the Upper Missouri*, 27, 36; Alexander, "Manuel Lisa"; Shepley, *Movers and Shakers, Scalawags and Suffragettes*, 92.
39. Fischer, "Osage and the Fur Trade"; Peterson, "Manuel Lisa's Warehouse," 59; Shelpley, *Movers and Shakers*, 92.
40. Fischer, "Osage and the Fur Trade"; Alexander, "Manuel Lisa"; Peterson, "Manuel Lisa's Warehouse," 60; Harper, "Manuel Lisa."
41. Peterson, "Manuel Lisa's Warehouse," 60; Corbett, *In Her Place*, 28; Winch, *Colored Aristocracy*, 23.

42. Peterson, "Manuel Lisa's Warehouse," 60; U.S. Congress, "Treaty with the Yankton Sioux, 1815."
43. Alexander, "Manuel Lisa"; Harper, "Manuel Lisa"; Peterson, "Manuel Lisa's Warehouse," 60.
44. Alexander, "Manuel Lisa"; Corbett, *In Her Place*, 31.
45. Corbett, *In Her Place*, 31; Peterson, "Manuel Lisa's Warehouse," 62–63.
46. Peterson, "Manuel Lisa's Warehouse," 63–65.
47. Andrews, *Shantyboats and Roustabouts*, 116–18, 124; John Williams, letter to the editor, *St. Louis Post-Dispatch*, October 7, 1907.
48. "Modern Structure Is to Replace an Old Landmark," *St. Louis Republic*, August 29, 1900; "Several Big Eastern Firms Lease Stores in St. Louis," *St. Louis Republic*, February 8, 1903; "Local and Suburban," *St. Louis Republic*, March 4, 1903; "Urge Action on Terminal Bills," *St. Louis Globe-Democrat*, May, 16 1903; and "Delegates Insist City Be Compensated," *St. Louis Post-Dispatch*, June 19, 1903.
49. Toft, "Arch Grounds and the Old Rock House"; Beulah Schacht, "Rock House Obituary Recalls Famous and Infamous," *St. Louis Globe-Democrat*, June 8, 1958; Peterson, "Manuel Lisa's Warehouse," 65; "Riverfront Night Life Gone Like Mark Twain's Steamers," *St. Louis Globe-Democrat*, July 9, 1939.
50. Toft, "Arch Grounds and the Old Rock House"; Peterson, "Manuel Lisa's Warehouse," 65.
51. Toft, "Arch Grounds and the Old Rock House."
52. Peterson, "Manuel Lisa's Warehouse," 66, 68, 71, 73.
53. "Part of City Jail to Use as Its Brig," *St. Louis Glove-Democrat*, February 9, 1945; Toft, "Arch Grounds and the Old Rock House."
54. Charles Van Ravenswaay, letter to the editor, *St. Louis Globe-Democrat*, May 24, 1958; "Workers Clearing Historic Site of Old Rock House," *Neighborhood News* (St. Louis, MO), August 6, 1959; E.F. Porter Jr., "Dismantled Landmark Missing," *St. Louis Post-Dispatch*, July 11, 1965; Peterson, "Manuel Lisa's Warehouse," 68; Toft, "Arch Grounds and the Old Rock House"; Porter, "Dismantled Landmark Missing."
55. Moore, "Resurrecting History in St. Louis."

Chapter 4

56. Slade, "Christmas Killing"; City of St. Louis, "Brief History of St. Louis"; Brown, *Stagolee Shot Billy*, 41.
57. Slade, "Christmas Killing."
58. "Criminal Capers," *St. Louis Post-Dispatch*, March 10, 1884; "Denison's Docket," *St. Louis Globe-Democrat*, November 19, 1884; "Second District

Police Court," *St. Louis Post-Dispatch*, August 21, 1885; "New Warrants," *St. Louis Post-Dispatch*, November 22, 1887; "Court of Correction," *St. Louis Globe-Democrat*, October 25, 1888; "New Warrants," *St. Louis Globe-Democrat*, May 17, 1889; "Court of Criminal Correction," *St. Louis Globe-Democrat*, September 23, 1890; "Court of Criminal Correction," *St. Louis Globe-Democrat*, September 27, 1890; "Held for Highway Robbery," *St. Louis Globe-Democrat*, February 6, 1892; "An Opium Joint Raided," *St. Louis Globe-Democrat*, September 10, 1894; "Fractured His Skull," *St. Louis Post-Dispatch*, November 13, 1894; "Fighting Negroes Arrested," *St. Louis Post-Dispatch*, January 21, 1895.

59. "Tragedy at a Picnic," *St. Louis Globe-Democrat*, June 16, 1887; "Local Brevities," *St. Louis Globe-Democrat*, May 7, 1889.

60. Brown, *Stagolee Shot Billy*, 38.

61. "Shot in Curtis' Place," *St. Louis Globe-Democrat*, December 26, 1895; "Result of a Feud," *St. Louis Post-Dispatch*, December 27, 1895.

62. Slade, "Christmas Killing"; Brown, *Stagolee Shot Billy*, 22; "Both May Die," *St. Louis Globe-Democrat*, August 20, 1897.

63. Olson, *That St. Louis Thing*, 1:48, 50; Blesh and Janis, *They All Played Ragtime*, 39; Brown, *Stagolee Shot Billy*, 23.

64. Olson, *That St. Louis Thing*, 1:50–53.

65. Ibid., 53; Brown, *Stagolee Shot Billy*, 24; "Sheldon's Victim Dies," *St. Louis Globe-Democrat*, December 27, 1895.

66. Brown, *Stagolee Shot Billy*, 25–26; "Coroner's Inquests," *St. Louis Globe-Democrat*, December 28, 1895.

67. "The Criminal Courts," *St. Louis Globe-Democrat*, June 26, 1896; "Stack Lee's Trial," *St. Louis Post-Dispatch*, July 13, 1896; "Shelton's Jury Disagreed," *St. Louis Post-Dispatch*, July 18, 1896; Brown, *Stagolee Shot Billy*, 33.

68. "On Trial for Murder," *St. Louis Post-Dispatch*, May 10, 1897; Brown, *Stagolee Shot Billy*, 63; "Lee Shelton Gets Twenty-Five Years," *St. Louis Globe-Democrat*, May 14, 1897; "Minor Criminal Matters," *St. Louis Globe-Democrat*, July 4, 1897; "Off for the Penitentiary," *St. Louis Post-Dispatch*, October 7, 1897.

69. "Two Negroes Pardoned Are in Cells Again," *St. Louis Post-Dispatch*, March 17, 1911; Brown, *Stagolee Shot Billy*, 33–34.

Chapter 5

70. Nester, *From Mountain Man to Millionaire*, 4–9.

71. Ibid, 9–11.

72. Ibid., 11–12.

73. Ibid., 17, 44, 46, 51, 54.

NOTES TO PAGES 42–49

74. Ibid., 98, 108, 110.

75. Ibid., 105, 112–13, 120–21.

76. Ibid., 123, 127–29.

77. Ibid., 129–32.

78. Ibid., 132, 142, 144.

79. Find a Grave, "Robert Campbell"; Nester, *From Mountain Man to Millionaire*, 149, 152.

80. Nester, *From Mountain Man to Millionaire*, 172, 175–76, 181.

81. Ibid., 177; Gordon, *Fire, Pestilence, and Death*, 26–30.

82. Gordon, *Fire, Pestilence, and Death*, 13–14; Nester, *From Mountain Man to Millionaire*, 184; Find a Grave, "Robert Campbell."

83. Nester, *From Mountain Man to Millionaire*, 185; Tim O'Neil, "May 17, 1849: The Great Fire that Changed the Face of St. Louis," *St. Louis Post-Dispatch*, May 17, 2023.

84. Nester, *From Mountain Man to Millionaire*, 188, 199.

85. Ibid., 190–92, 195; U.S. Congress, "Treaty of Fort Laramie with Sioux, ETC., 1851."

86. Nester, *From Mountain Man to Millionaire*, 197–98; Kolk, *Taking Possession*, 23–25.

87. Find a Grave, "Robert Campbell"; Nester, *From Mountain Man to Millionaire*, 198–99, 222, 228; Campbell House Museum, "Campbell Family"; Haines, "Fertility and Mortality."

88. Nester, *From Mountain Man to Millionaire*, 21; U.S. Senate, "Crittenden Compromise"; Campbell House Museum, "Slavery"; Nester, *From Mountain Man to Millionaire*, 136–37.

89. Nester, *From Mountain Man to Millionaire*, 212, 224, 227.

90. Ibid., 213; Robert Campbell Loyalty Oath (D08514), courtesy of the Missouri Historical Society, St. Louis, 1863; "Rebuild the Southern," *St. Louis Post-Dispatch*, April 11, 1877.

91. Campbell House Museum, "Campbell House"; "Campbell Family"; Nester, *From Mountain Man to Millionaire*, 228.

92. Nester, *From Mountain Man to Millionaire*, 228.

93. "Tombs of Fire," *St. Louis Daily Globe-Democrat*, April 11, 1877.

94. "The Most Deserving Among the Suffers by the Southern Hotel Fire," *St. Louis Globe-Democrat*, April 15, 1877; "No Testimonial Could Be More Worthily," *St. Louis Globe-Democrat*, April 19, 1877; "Building Talk," *St. Louis Daily Globe-Democrat*, April 29, 1877; Nester, *From Mountain Man to Millionaire*, 250–51.

95. Nester, *From Mountain Man to Millionaire*, 251; Kavanaugh, *Campbell Family of St. Louis*, 24; Kolk, *Taking Possession*, 38; Campbell House Museum, "Campbell Family."

96. Nester, *From Mountain Man to Millionaire*, 252; Campbell House Museum, "Campbell Family"; Kolk, *Taking Possession*, 45.
97. Kolk, *Taking Possession*, 38–40; Campbell House Museum, "Campbell Family."
98. Kolk, *Taking Possession*, 40; Nester, *From Mountain Man to Millionaire*, 252.
99. Nester, *From Mountain Man to Millionaire*, 252; *Campbell House Courier*, "Campbell House Marks 65 Years," 3.
100. Campbell House Museum, "Campbell House."
101. Crone, "Campbell House Mysteries."

Chapter 6

102. "Capt. Bissell's House Measured by Historic Homes Survey," *St. Louis Globe-Democrat*, February 18, 1940; "Bissell Mansion Destined to Make Room for Mark Twain Expressway," *St. Louis Globe-Democrat*, November 2, 1958.
103. *St. Louis Globe-Democrat*, "Capt. Bissell's House Measured"; Fisher, "Treaties of Portage Des Sioux," 499–500; U.S. Department of the Interior, National Park Service, "Captain Lewis Bissell Mansion."
104. Swekosky, "Captain Lewis Bissell Mansion"; Find a Grave, "Lewis Bissell."
105. Weil, "Bissell Mansion," 1; Find a Grave, "Lewis Bissell."
106. Weil, "Bissell Mansion," 6; Brean, "Memory and Mourning"; Find a Grave, "Lewis Bissell."
107. Tim O'Neil, "Nov. 1, 1855: A Bridge Disaster Derails St. Louis Dream for a Transcontinental Railroad," *St. Louis Post-Dispatch*, November 1, 2023; Swekosky, "Captain Lewis Bissell Mansion"; O'Neil, "Nov. 1, 1855."
108. Weil, "Bissell Mansion," 6; Swekosky, "Captain Lewis Bissell Mansion."
109. Swekosky, "Captain Lewis Bissell Mansion"; Weil, "Bissell Mansion," 6.
110. *St. Louis Globe-Democrat*, "Bissell Mansion Destined."
111. "Effort to Save Bissell Mansion Will Be Made," *St. Louis Globe-Democrat*, November 8, 1958; Frank T. Hilliker, letter to the editor, "Regrettable Razing of Bissell Mansion," *St. Louis Globe-Democrat*, November 24, 1858; Weil, "Bissell Mansion," 6.
112. Weil, "Bissell Mansion," 6.
113. Valerie Schremp Hahn, "1820s Bissell Mansion, Longtime Dinner Theater Venue, Is for Sale for $250,000," *St. Louis Post-Dispatch*, August 11, 2022.

Chapter 7

114. Cappel, "Abandoned Hospital Complex."

115. Prietto, "Journey of the Sisters of Charity," 33.

116. Ibid., 28, 33–35; Cappel, "Abandoned Hospital Complex."

117. Cappel, "Abandoned Hospital Complex"; Grass, "Shaper of Cities"; Gordon, *Fire, Pestilence, and Death*, 13.

118. "Mayor Message," *St. Louis Glove-Democrat*, May 16, 1855.

119. "Destructive Fire," *Daily Missouri Republican*, May 16, 1856; Cappel, "Abandoned Hospital Complex."

120. "Board of Delegates," *Daily Missouri Republican*, February 10, 1858.

121. Cappel, "Abandoned Hospital Complex"; "City Hospital Demolished," *St. Louis Globe-Democrat*, May 28, 1896.

122. "City Hospital Building Loses Sections of Plaster and Fast Falling to Pieces," *St. Louis Post-Dispatch*, August 6, 1900.

123. "City of Sick Is Moved into Its New Home," *St. Louis Post-Dispatch*, August 10, 1905; Cappel, "Abandoned Hospital Complex."

124. Cappel, "Abandoned Hospital Complex."

125. American Influenza Epidemic of 1918–1919, "St. Louis, Missouri."

126. Ibid.; Tim O'Neil, "A Look Back: Aggressive Measures Helped Hold Down Number of Deaths from 1918 Spanish Flu," *St. Louis Post-Dispatch*, November 4, 2023.

127. Cappel, "Abandoned Hospital Complex."

128. Ibid.

129. Ibid.

130. Ibid.; City of St. Louis, "Brownfield Success Story."

Chapter 8

131. Orrmont, *James Buchanan Eads*, 7–10.

132. Ibid., 10–14.

133. Ibid., 18–21, 21, 29.

134. Ibid., 31–33, 36–37.

135. Ibid., 40, 42, 47–50; Shepley, *Movers and Shakers*, 68.

136. Orrmont, *James Buchanan Eads*, 65.

137. "Proceedings in the Senate," *Macomb (IL) Weekly Journal*, January 13, 1865; "Senate," *Alton (IL) Telegraph*, March 30, 1866; John M. Krum, "Letter from John M. Krum," *Daily Missouri Republican*, February 17, 1867; Jas B. Eads, "Bridging the Mississippi," *Daily Missouri Republican*, April 19, 1866.

138. Orrmont, *James Buchanan Eads*, 67; "St. Louis Bridge," *Daily Missouri Republican*, February 19, 1867.
139. "Local News: The Proposed Bridge Across the Mississippi," *Daily Missouri Republican*, February 17, 1867; Orrmont, *James Buchanan Eads*, 70–71; "The Bridge at St. Louis," *Daily Missouri Republican*, February 19, 1867.
140. L.B. Boomer, "The Illinois and St. Louis Bridge Company," *Daily Missouri Republican*, November 26, 1867; "One Hundred Thousand Cubic Yards of Stone," *Daily Missouri Republican*, July 18, 1867; "The Mississippi Bridge," *Daily Missouri Republican*, August 4, 1867; "The Bridge at Washington Avenue," *Daily Missouri Republican*, September 30, 1867.
141. D.R. Garrison, "The Mississippi Bridge," *Daily Missouri Republican*, December 11, 1867; "The Bridge Question," *Daily Missouri Republican*, December 27, 1867; "The Bridge Controversy at an End," *Daily Missouri Republican*, March 7, 1868.
142. Orrmont, *James Buchanan Eads*, 71–72, 74–75; "The Mississippi Bridge," *Daily Missouri Republican*, August 4, 1867.
143. Orrmont, *James Buchanan Eads*, 77; Butler, "Caisson Disease," 449; Corporation for Public Broadcasting, "Building a Bridge Pier."
144. "The Progress of the Bridge," *Missouri Republican*, February 24, 1870; "Work on the Bridge," *Missouri Republican*, February 26, 1870; "Inquest at City Hospital," *Missouri Republican*, March 25, 1870.
145. Butler, "Caisson Disease," 449–51; *Missouri Republican*, "Inquest at City Hospital."
146. Butler, "Caisson Disease," 450; *Missouri Republican*, "Inquest at City Hospital."
147. Butler, "Caisson Disease," 452, 454, 456.
148. "Terrible Tornado," *Missouri Republican*, March 9, 1871; "The East Abutment," *Missouri Republican*, March 17, 1871.
149. James B. Eads, "The Bridge: Progress of the Work Report of the Chief Engineer," *Missouri Republican*, May 13, 1871; Orrmont, *James Buchanan Eads*, 87.
150. Eads, "The Bridge"; James B. Eads, "Illinois and St. Louis Bridge Company: Report of the Chief Engineer, October, 1871," *Missouri Republican*, December 10, 1871.
151. Eads, "Illinois and St. Louis Bridge Company: Report."
152. "The Illinois and St. Louis Bridge," *Chicago Evening Post*, January 19, 1872; "The Bridge," *Missouri Republican*, February 25, 1872; "Fighting the St. Louis Bridge," *St. Joseph (MO) Gazette*, July 26, 1873; "St. Louis Bridge," *Missouri Republican*, August 22, 1873; "The Bridge and 'Canal'," *Missouri Republican*, October 20, 1873; "That Canal," *St. Louis Republican*, November 19, 1873.

153. "The Bridge and the Right of Navigation," *St. Louis Republican*, April 16, 1874; Orrmont, *James Buchanan Eads*, 97; "Washington: Bridge Reports Consigned to Pigeon-Holes," *St. Louis Republican*, April 19, 1874.
154. "Office Illinois and St. Louis Bridge Co.: The Bridge," *St. Louis Republican*, April 19, 1874; Orrmont, *James Buchanan Eads*, 101; "The Opening," *St. Louis Post-Dispatch*, May 23, 1874; "The Latest News," *Daily Journal of Commerce* (Kansas City, MO), May 27, 1874.
155. "St. Louis Bridge Was Formerly Opened," *Daily Tribune* (Jefferson City, MO), June 6, 1874; "The Bridge: The Elephant Declares It a Good Piece of Work," *St. Louis Republican*, June 15, 1874; Orrmont, *James Buchanan Eads*, 105; "Putting on the Weight," *St. Louis Post-Dispatch*, July 2, 1874.
156. "Gloria! 1776–1874," *St. Louis Republican*, July 5, 1874; Moore, *Old Courthouse*, 11; "Wind's Deadly Work," *St. Louis Globe-Democrat*, May 28, 1896; Tim O'Neil, "It All Happened in 20 Minutes: The Greatest Single-Day Catastrophe to Hit St. Louis," *St. Louis Post-Dispatch*, May 28, 2023; Ken Leiser, "Stimulus Spurs Eads Work $25 Million Will Be Spent on Bridge, Largely to Rehab MetroLink line," *St. Louis Post-Dispatch*, October 12, 2009.

Chapter 9

157. Primm, *Lion of the Valley*, 62; Chatillon-DeMenil Mansion Foundation, "Chatillon Family"; Parkman, *Oregon Trail*, 16–17.
158. Parkman, *Oregon Trail*, 15, 17.
159. Chatillon-DeMenil Mansion Foundation, "Chatillon Family"; Koster, "Henri Chatillon's Heart of Lightness"; Parkman, *Oregon Trail*, 142.
160. Parkman, *Oregon Trail*, 165–68. Find a Grave, "Emily Lessert."
161. Koster, "Henri Chatillon's Heart of Lightness."
162. Ibid.; Chatillon-DeMenil Mansion Foundation, "Chatillon Family"; Find a Grave, "Emily Lessert."
163. Chatillon-DeMenil Mansion Foundation, "DeMenil Family"; Hurt, "Chouteau, Auguste Pierre."
164. Hyde and Conard, *Encyclopedia of the History of St. Louis*, 1:552; Kurtz and Kramer, "Chatillon-DeMenil House National Register of Historical Places Inventory—Nomination Form," Item #8, 2; Find a Grave, "Henry Nicolas DeMenil."
165. Hyde and Conard, *Encyclopedia of the History of St. Louis*, 1:553; U.S. Department of the Interior, National Park Service, *Chatillon-DeMenil House*, 8:2; Chatillon-DeMenil Mansion Foundation, "DeMenil Family."
166. Hyde and Conard, *Encyclopedia of the History of St. Louis*, 1:552–53; Drumm, "Memoirs of Deceased Members," 199.

NOTES TO PAGES 81–89

167. Hammerman, "Cherokee Cave."
168. Chatillon-DeMenil Mansion Foundation, "DeMenil Family"; U.S. Department of the Interior, National Park Service, *Chatillon-DeMenil House*, 8:3; "St. Louis in Splinters," *St. Louis Globe-Democrat*, July 10, 1876.
169. Hyde and Conard, *Encyclopedia of the History of St. Louis*, 1:552; *St. Louis Magazine*, "When Did St. Louis Magazine Really Start?," March 16, 2017; Find a Grave, "Henry Nicolas DeMenil."
170. Chatillon-DeMenil Mansion Foundation, "DeMenil Family"; *St. Louis Magazine*, "When Did St. Louis Magazine Really Start?"
171. Drumm, "Memoirs of Deceased Members," 200–201; Chatillon-DeMenil Mansion Foundation, "DeMenil Family"; *St. Louis Magazine*, "When Did St. Louis Magazine Really Start?"
172. Drumm, "Memoirs of Deceased Members," 201; Chatillon-DeMenil Mansion Foundation, "Our Collection"; Sonderman and Truax, *St. Louis*, 7–8.
173. Drumm, "Memoirs of Deceased Members," 200; Chatillon-DeMenil Mansion Foundation, "DeMenil Family."
174. Drumm, "Memoirs of Deceased Members," 200; U.S. Department of the Interior, National Park Service, *Chatillon-DeMenil House*, 8:3.
175. U.S. Department of the Interior, National Park Service, *Chatillon-DeMenil House*, 8:3–4; Chatillon-DeMenil Mansion Foundation, "Cherokee Cave & Museum"; Simpson, "Bones in the Brewery."
176. Chatillon-DeMenil Mansion, "Cherokee Cave."
177. U.S. Department of the Interior, National Park Service, *Chatillon-DeMenil House*, 8:4.
178. Koster, "Henri Chatillon's Heart of Lightness."

Chapter 10

179. Walker, *Lemp*, 2.
180. Naffziger, "Unveiling the Real Johann Adam Lemp."
181. Walker, *Lemp*, 2, 4–5.
182. Ibid., 2, 12.
183. Naffziger, "Unveiling the Real Johann Adam Lemp"; Walker, *Lemp*, 6; Naffziger, "Lemps, the Braunecks, and the Secrets of Lot 36"; Naffziger, "Who Was William J. Lemp Sr."
184. Walker, *Lemp*, 8.
185. Ibid., 8–10, 15; Taylor, *Haunted St. Louis*, 183–84.
186. Taylor, *Haunted St. Louis*, 182–84; Walker, *Lemp*, 44, 113; Pittman, *History and Haunting of Lemp Mansion*, 48.
187. Walker, *Lemp*, 37; Taylor, *Haunted St. Louis*, 186.

188. Taylor, *Haunted St. Louis*, 186; Walker, *Lemp*, 37–38.

189. Walker, *Lemp*, 38; Taylor, *Haunted St. Louis*, 187.

190. Walker, *Lemp*, 29–32, 44.

191. Pittman, *History and Haunting of Lemp Mansion*, 238; Taylor, *Haunted St. Louis*, 191; "Live Birds Fed to Monkeys, 'Lavender Lady' Says in Suit," *St. Louis Post-Dispatch*, March 19, 1908.

192. Pittman, *History and Haunting of Lemp Mansion*, 247; "Lemp Objected to All Lavender Gowns for Wife," *St. Louis Post-Dispatch*, February 15, 1909; Walker, *Lemp*, 63.

193. Walker, *Lemp*, 49–51, 68; "Lemp Rejoices at Divorce for Lavender Lady," *St. Louis Post-Dispatch*, February 18, 1909.

194. Walker, *Lemp*, 69–71.

195. Ibid., 74–75; U.S. Senate, *National Prohibition Act*.

196. Walker, *Lemp*, 74–75.

197. Pittman, *History and Haunting of Lemp Mansion*, 125–26; Walker, *Lemp*, 77.

198. Pittman, *History and Haunting of Lemp Mansion*, 300–302; Walker, *Lemp*, 80.

199. Walker, *Lemp*, 80, 82–83; Pittman, *History and Haunting of Lemp Mansion*, 302.

200. Pittman, *History and Haunting of Lemp Mansion*, 305; Walker, *Lemp*, 81.

201. Walker, *Lemp*, 84; Pittman, *History and Haunting of Lemp Mansion*, 318–19.

202. Walker, *Lemp*, 86–88.

203. Ibid., 89; Taylor, *Haunted St. Louis*, 207.

204. Pittman, *History and Haunting of Lemp Mansion*, 343, 345, 347; Walker, *Lemp*, 89–90.

205. Walker, *Lemp*, 89.

206. Ibid., 100, 108; Taylor, *Haunted St. Louis*, 209.

207. Taylor, *Haunted St. Louis*, 210–12.

Chapter 11

208. Archdiocese of St. Louis, "1818–1843."

209. Ibid.; Byrnes, *Always at the Frontier*, 8; Honors Crossroads 2016, "History of St. Louis: 1818–1888."

210. Byrnes, *Always at the Frontier*, 22–23; Saint Louis University, "Saint Louis University Timeline."

211. Saint Louis University, "Saint Louis University Timeline."

212. Allen, *Possessed*, 10, 43, 245–48.

213. Ibid., 6, 11–12, 24.

214. Ibid., 3, 6, 40.

215. Ibid., *Possessed*, 43–46; Taylor, *Devil Came to St. Louis*, 62.

216. Taylor, *Devil Came to St. Louis*, 48–49, 55.

217. Ibid., 55–57, 59, 61–62.
218. Ibid., 50–52.
219. Ibid., 63–64, 74.
220. Allen, *Possessed*, 128; Taylor, *Devil Came to St. Louis*, 68–71.
221. Allen, *Possessed*, 78, 85, 91; Taylor, *Devil Came to St. Louis*, 81–82.
222. Allen, *Possessed*, 91–93, 255–57; Taylor, *Devil Came to St. Louis*, 85.
223. Allen, *Possessed*, 257–259.
224. Ibid., 134, 259–64; Taylor, *Devil Came to St. Louis*, 99–101.
225. Allen, *Possessed*, 139–40, 265–68.
226. Ibid., 142, 149–50, 267.
227. Ibid., 268–70.
228. Ibid., 270–71.
229. Ibid., 271–73.
230. Ibid., 275–77, 279.
231. Ibid., 186, 279–85, 289.
232. Ibid., 289; Taylor, *Devil Came to St. Louis*, 147.
233. Yang, "Boy Whose Case Inspired the Exorcist."
234. Garland, "Exorcism Exposé."
235. Ibid.; Allen, *Possessed*, xiii–xiv.

BIBLIOGRAPHY

Alexander, Kathy. "Manuel Lisa: Expert on the Missouri River." Legends of America, September 2023, https://www.legendsofamerica.com/we-manuellisa.

Allen, Thomas B. *Possessed: The True Story of an Exorcism*. San Jose, CA: iUniverse.com Inc., 2000.

American Influenza Epidemic of 1918–1919: A Digital Encyclopedia. "St. Louis, Missouri." http://www.influenzaarchive.org.

Andrews, Gregg. *Shantyboats and Roustabouts: The River Poor of St. Louis, 1875–1930*. Baton Rouge: Louisiana State University Press, 2023.

Archdiocese of St. Louis. "1818–1843: The Beginnings of a Catholic City." https://www.archstl.org/history/beginnings.

Blesh, Rudi, and Harriet Janis. *They All Played Ragtime: The True Story of an American Music*. New York: Alfred A. Knopf, 1950.

Brean, Dawn Reid. "Memory and Mourning: Death in the Gilded Age." Frick Pittsburgh Museums and Gardens, September 19, 2019. https://www.thefrickpittsburgh.org/Story-Memory-and-Mourning-Death-in-the-Gilded-Age.

Brown, Cecil. *Stagolee Shot Billy*. Cambridge, MA: Harvard University Press, 2003.

Butler, W.P. "Caisson Disease During the Construction of the Eads and Brooklyn Bridges: A Review." *Undersea and Hyperbaric Medical Society, Inc.* 31 no. 4 (2004): 445–59.

Byrnes, Dolores M. *Always at the Frontier: Saint Louis University, 1818–2018*. St. Louis, MO: Saint Louis University Press, 2017.

Campbell House Courier. "Campbell House Marks 65 Years as a Museum" (Spring 2009): 3. Campbell House Museum https://www.campbellhousemuseum.org/wp-content/uploads/2013/08/newsletterS09.pdf.

Campbell House Museum. "Campbell Family." June 5, 2013. https://campbellhousemuseum.wordpress.com/about/campbell-family.

———. "Campbell House." June 5, 2013. https://campbellhousemuseum.wordpress.com/about/campbell-house.

———. "Slavery: A Complicated Story." February 25, 2015. https://campbellhousemuseum.wordpress.com/2015/02/25/slavery-a-complicated-story.

Cappel, Bill. "Abandoned Hospital Complex in Saint Louis." Historic Structures. https://www.historic-structures.com/mo/st_louis/city-hospital.

Chatillon-DeMenil Mansion Foundation. "The Chatillon Family." https://www.demenil.org/chatillon-family.

———. "The Cherokee Cave & Museum of Natural History." https://www.demenil.org/cherokee-cave.

———. "The DeMenil Family." https://www.demenil.org/demenil-family.

———. "Our Collection: 1904 World's Fair Collection." https://www.demenil.org/exhibits.

City of St. Louis. "A Brief History of St. Louis." https://www.stlouis-mo.gov/visit-play/stlouis-history.cfm#.

———. "Brownfield Success Story." https://www.stlouis-mo.gov/government/departments/sldc/brownfields/City-Hospital.cfm.

Corbett, Katharine T. *In Her Place: A Guide to St. Louis Women's History.* St. Louis: Missouri History Society Press, 1999.

Corporation for Public Broadcasting. "Building a Bridge Pier." American Experience. https://www.pbs.org/wgbh/americanexperience/features/eads-building-bridge-pier.

Crone, Thomas. "The Campbell House Mysteries: The Case of the Hidden Half-Dollars." *St. Louis Magazine* (December 26, 2011). https://www.stlmag.com/culture/The-Campbell-House-Mysteries-The-Case-of-the-Hidden-Half-Dollars.

Drumm, Stella M. "Memoirs of Deceased Members: Dr. Alexander Nicholas DeMenil." Missouri Historical Society Collections 6 no. 2 (February 1929): 199–204.

Find a Grave Database. "Emily Lessert." https://www.findagrave.com/memorial/82863123/emily-lessert.

———. "Henry Nicolas DeMenil." https://www.findagrave.com/memorial/48362718/henry-nicolas-demenil.

———. "Lewis Bissell." https://www.findagrave.com/memorial/18501/lewis-bissell.

———. "Robert Campbell." https://www.findagrave.com/memorial/94873777/robert-campbell.

Fischer, William, Jr. "The Osage and the Fur Trade." Historical Marker Database, June 16, 2016. https://www.hmdb.org/m.asp?m=61382.

Fisher, Robert L. "The Treaties of Portage Des Sioux." *Mississippi Valley Historical Review* 19, no. 4 (March 1933): 495–508.

Foley, William E. "Auguste Chouteau (1749?–1829)." Missouri Encyclopedia, The State Historical Society of Missouri, January 24, 2023. https://missouriencyclopedia.org/people/chouteau-auguste.

———. "John B.C. Lucas (1758–1842)." Missouri Encyclopedia, The State Historical Society of Missouri, July 14, 2022. https://missouriencyclopedia.org/people/lucas-john-b-c.

Garland, Amy. "Exorcism Exposé." *Universitas Magazine* (Spring 2014). Saint Louis University. https://www.slu.edu/universitas/archive/2014/exorcism.php.

Gesley, Jenny. "Old Courthouse in St. Louis, MO—Pic of the Week." Library of Congress Blogs, June 2, 2017. https://blogs.loc.gov/law/2017/06/old-courthouse-in-st-louis-mo-pic-of-the-week.

Goodwin, Cardinal. "A Larger View of the Yellowstone Expedition, 1819–1820." *Mississippi Valley Historical Review* 4. no. 3 (December 1917): 299–313.

Gordon, Christopher Alan. *Fire, Pestilence, and Death: St. Louis 1849*. St. Louis: Missouri Historical Society Press, 2018.

Grass, Jim. "A Shaper of Cities: St. Louis and Cholera, 1849." Story Maps Arcgis, April 26, 2022. https://storymaps.arcgis.com/stories/c95416086d0b4b8399f8d86c1f187c41/print.

Haines, Michael. "Fertility and Mortality in the United States." Economic History Association. https://eh.net/encyclopedia/fertility-and-mortality-in-the-united-states.

Hammerman, Harley. "Cherokee Cave." LostSTL. https://www.loststl.com/cherokee/cherokee.htm.

Harper, Kimberly. "Manuel Lisa." Historic Missourians, State Historical Society of Missouri. https://historicmissourians.shsmo.org/manuel-lisa.

Hebrank, Arthur W. *The Geologic Story of the St. Louis Riverfront: A Walking Tour*. Rolla: Missouri Department of Natural Resources Division of Geology and Land Survey, 1989.

Honors Crossroads 2016: Living the Jesuit Mission. "A History of St. Louis: 1818–1888." 2023. https://livingthejesuitmission.wordpress.com/group-1.

Hurt, Douglas A. "Chouteau, Auguste Pierre (1786–1838)." Encyclopedia of Oklahoma History and Culture Oklahoma Historical Society. https://www.okhistory.org/publications/enc/entry.php?entry=CH057.

Hyde, William, and Howard Louis Conard. *Encyclopedia of the History of St. Louis: A Compendium of History and Biography for Ready Reference*. Vol. 1. Madison, WI: Southern History Company, 1899.

Institute of Museum and Library Services Missouri State Library. "Missouri Drake Constitution Ratified." Civil War on the Western Border: The Missouri-Kansas Conflict, 1855–65. https://civilwaronthewesternborder. org/timeline/missouri-drake-constitution-ratified.

Kavanaugh, Maureen O'Connor. *The Campbell Family of St. Louis: Their Public Triumphs and Personal Tragedies*. St. Louis, MO: Campbell House Foundation, 2016.

Kolk, Heidi Aronson. *Taking Possession: The Politics of Memory in a St. Louis Town House*. Amherst: University of Massachusetts Press, 2019.

Koster, John. "Henri Chatillon's Heart of Lightness." HistoryNet, November 25, 2015. https://www.historynet.com/henri-chatillons-heart-of-lightness.

Kurtz, Katherine Neilson, and Gerhardt Kramer. "Chatillon-DeMenil House National Register of Historical Places Inventory—Nomination Form." St. Louis, Missouri, 1977. U.S. Department of the Interior, National Park Service. https://mostateparks.com/sites/mostateparks/files/Chatillon-Demenil%20House.pdf.

Moore, Bob. "Resurrecting History in St. Louis." Gateway Arch Park Foundation, February 14, 2018. https://www.archpark.org/updates/blog/resurrecting-history-in-st-louis.

Moore, Robert J. *The Old Courthouse*. St. Louis: Jefferson National Parks Association, 2004.

Naffziger, Chris. "How Adam Lemp Laid the Foundation of One of the Greatest Breweries in America." *St. Louis Magazine* (August 6, 2020). https://www.stlmag.com/history/adam-lemp.

———. "The Lemps, the Braunecks, and the Secrets of Lot 36." *St. Louis Magazine* (August 30, 2017). https://www.stlmag.com/history/profiles/the-lemps-the-braunecks-and-the-secrets-of-lot-36.

———. "Unveiling the Real Johann Adam Lemp." *St. Louis Magazine* (August 2, 2017). https://www.stlmag.com/history/profiles/unveiling-the-real-johann-adam-lemp.

———. "Who Was William J. Lemp Sr., One of the Heirs of Adam Lemp." *St. Louis Magazine* (August 28, 2020). https://www.stlmag.com/history/william-lemp-sr.

Nester, William R. *From Mountain Man to Millionaire: The Bold and Dashing Life of Robert Campbell.* Columbia: University of Missouri Press, 2011.

Olson, Bruce R. *That St. Louis Thing.* Vol. 1, *An American Story of Roots, Rhythm and Race.* Morrisville, NC: Lulu Publishing Services, 2016.

Orrmont, Arthur. *James Buchanan Eads: The Man Who Mastered the Mississippi.* Englewood Cliffs, NJ: Rutledge Books Inc., 1970.

Parkman, Francis. *The Oregon Trail: Sketches of Prairie and Rocky-mountain Life.* Boston, MA: Little, Brown, 1927.

Peterson, Charles E. "Manuel Lisa's Warehouse." *Bulletin of the Missouri Historical Society* 4, no. 2 (January 1948): 59–73.

Pittman, Rebecca F. *The History and Haunting of Lemp Mansion.* Loveland, CO: Wonderland Productions Inc., 2015.

Prietto, Carole. "The Journey of the Sisters of Charity to St. Louis, 1828." *Confluence: Undergraduate Research Journal of Lindenwood University* (Spring/Summer 2010).

Primm, James Neal. *Lion of the Valley: St. Louis, Missouri, 1764–1980.* St. Louis: Missouri Historical Society Press, 1998.

Saint Louis University. "Saint Louis University Timeline." https://www.slu.edu/timeline.

Shepley, Carol Ferring. *Movers and Shakers, Scalawags and Suffragettes: Tales from Bellefontaine Cemetery.* St. Louis: Missouri Historical Society Press, 2015.

Simmons, David J. "Henry Singleton's Architectural Legacy in St. Louis." *Society of Architectural Historians Missouri Valley Chapter Newsletter* 14, no. 1B (Spring 2008): 5–10.

Simpson, George Gaylord. "Bones in the Brewery: A Paleontologist's Rendezvous with History and Prehistory in St. Louis." *Natural History* (June 1946). https://www.naturalhistorymag.com/htmlsite/master.html?https://www.naturalhistorymag.com/htmlsite/editors_pick/1946_06_pick.html.

Slade, Paul. "A Christmas Killing: Stagger Lee." Planetslade. http://www.planetslade.com/stagger-lee.html.

Sonderman, Joe, and Mike Truax. *St. Louis: The 1904 World's Fair.* Charleston, SC: Arcadia Publishing, 2008.

Swekosky, William G., memorandum. "Captain Lewis Bissell Mansion." January 6, 1957. Swekosky Notre Dame College Collection, St. Louis County Residences, SNDC 5-01-001-0501-063, Missouri Historical Society.

Taylor, Troy. *The Devil Came to St. Louis: The True Story of the 1949 Exorcism.* Decatur, IL: Whitechapel Press, 2014.

———. *Haunted St. Louis: History and Hauntings Along the Mississippi.* 2nd ed. Jacksonville, IL: American Hauntings Ink, 2018.

Toft, Carolyn Hewes. "The Arch Grounds and the Old Rock House." *Newsletter of the Landmarks Association of St. Louis, Inc.* 31, no. 1 (January/ February 1996).

Truteau, Jean-Baptiste. *A Fur Trader on the Upper Missouri: The Journal and Description of Jean-Baptiste Truteau, 1794–1796.* Translated by Raymond J. DeMallie, Robert Vezina and Mildred Mott Wedel. Lincoln: University of Nebraska Press, 2017.

U.S. Congress. "Treaty of Fort Laramie with Sioux, ETC., 1851." September 17, 1851. *United States Statutes at Large* 11 Stat 749:594–96.

———. "Treaty with the Yankton Sioux, 1815." July 19, 1815, *United States Statues at Large* 7 Stat. 128:115.

U.S. Department of the Interior, National Park Service. "Captain Lewis Bissell Mansion: Historic American Buildings Survey." F. Ray Leimkuehler, St. Louis, Missouri, 1940. https://www.loc.gov/item/ mo0065.

U.S. Senate. "The Crittenden Compromise." https://www.senate.gov/ artandhistory/history/minute/Crittenden_Compromise.htm.

———. *National Prohibition Act,* HR 6810, 66th Cong., 1st sess. *Congressional Record* 58, no 8 (October 27, 1919): S 7,633–34.

Wagner, Dennis. "1818 James Monroe—The Yellowstone Expedition." State of the Union History, April 5, 2017. https://www. stateoftheunionhistory.com/2017/04/1818-james-monroe-yellowstone-expedition.html.

Walker, Stephen P. *Lemp: The Haunting History.* 2nd ed. St. Louis, MO: Mulligan Printing Company, 2014.

Weil, Andrew. "Bissell Mansion, 4426 Randall Place." *Newsletter of the Landmarks Association of St. Louis, Inc.* 51, no 1 (2016): 1–6.

Winch, Julie. *The Clamorgans: One Family's History of Race in America.* New York: Hill and Wang, 2011.

———. *The Colored Aristocracy of St. Louis by Cyprian Clamorgan.* Columbia: University of Missouri Press, 1999.

Yang, Maya. "Boy Whose Case Inspired the Exorcist Is Named by US Magazine." *The Guardian,* December 20, 2021. https://www. theguardian.com/us-news/2021/dec/20/the-exorcist-boy-named-magazine.

ABOUT THE AUTHOR

J ennifer Elwyn was encouraged early in life to embrace her curiosity and seek to find her own answers to the strange questions of the world around her. She grew up in the small village of Kaskaskia, Illinois, and later moved to the "big city" of St. Louis. She has a bachelor's degree in English from SIU Carbondale and a Master of Social Work degree from Saint Louis University. She writes a blog titled *Investigative Curiosity* that explores what it means to be a paranormal investigator while working full time for the neuroscience program at Saint Louis University.

FREE eBOOK OFFER

Scan the QR code below, enter your e-mail address and get our original Haunted America compilation eBook delivered straight to your inbox for free.

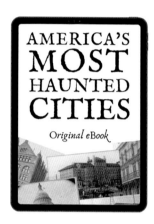

ABOUT THE BOOK

Every city, town, parish, community and school has their own paranormal history. Whether they are spirits caught in the Bardo, ancestors checking on their descendants, restless souls sending a message or simply spectral troublemakers, ghosts have been part of the human tradition from the beginning of time.

In this book, we feature a collection of stories from five of America's most haunted cities: Baltimore, Chicago, Galveston, New Orleans and Washington, D.C.

SCAN TO GET
AMERICA'S MOST HAUNTED CITIES

Having trouble scanning? Go to:
biz.arcadiapublishing.com/americas-most-haunted-cities